YORK NOTES

Nineteenth Century Short Stories

Notes by Sarah Rowbotham

 Longman   York Press

YORK PRESS
322 Old Brompton Road, London SW5 9JH

ADDISON WESLEY LONGMAN LIMITED
Edinburgh Gate, Harlow,
Essex CM20 2JE, United Kingdom
Associated companies, branches and representatives throughout the world

First published 1997

ISBN 0-582-31450-X

Design by Vicki Pacey, Trojan Horse
Illustrated by Chris Price
Phototypeset by Gem Graphics, Trenance, Mawgan Porth, Cornwall
Produced by Longman Asia Limited, Hong Kong

CONTENTS

Preface   4

PART ONE

INTRODUCTION   How to Study a Short Story   5
               Context & Setting   6

PART TWO

SUMMARIES   Detailed Summaries, Comment,
               Glossaries & Tests   8
               I   Togetherness ?   8
               II Making Choices   18
               III Women Amongst Men   27
               IV Outsiders   36
               V   Mystery and Detection   48

PART THREE

COMMENTARY   Themes   56
               Chronology   68
               Historical Perspective of the Story   70
               Structure   73
               Language & Style   75

PART FOUR

STUDY SKILLS   How to Use Quotations   77
               Essay Writing   78
               Sample Essay Plan & Questions   81

PART FIVE

CULTURAL CONNECTIONS
               Broader Perspectives   84
Literary Terms   85
Test Answers   86

PREFACE

York Notes are designed to give you a broader perspective on works of literature studied at GCSE and equivalent levels. We have carried out extensive research into the needs of the modern literature student prior to publishing this new edition. Our research showed that no existing series fully met students' requirements. Rather than present a single authoritative approach, we have provided alternative viewpoints, empowering students to reach their own interpretations of the text. York Notes provide a close examination of the work and include biographical and historical background, summaries, glossaries, analyses of characters, themes, structure and language, cultural connections and literary terms.

If you look at the Contents page you will see the structure for the series. However, there's no need to read from the beginning to the end as you would with a novel, play, poem or short story. Use the Notes in the way that suits you. Our aim is to help you with your understanding of the work, not to dictate how you should learn.

York Notes are written by English teachers and examiners, with an expert knowledge of the subject. They show you how to succeed in coursework and examination assignments, guiding you through the text and offering practical advice. Questions and comments will extend, test and reinforce your knowledge. Attractive colour design and illustrations improve clarity and understanding, making these Notes easy to use and handy for quick reference.

York Notes are ideal for:
• Essay writing
• Exam preparation
• Class discussion

The author of these Notes, Sarah Rowbotham, is an assistant examiner for GCSE English and English Literature. She teaches English at a large comprehensive school in Rotherham.

The text used in these Notes is *The New Windmill Book of Nineteenth Century Short Stories* edited by Mike Hamlin, Christine Hall and Jane Browne (Heinemann, 1992).

Health Warning: **This study guide will enhance your understanding, but should not replace the reading of the original text and/or study in class.**

PART ONE

INTRODUCTION

HOW TO STUDY A SHORT STORY

You have bought this book because you wanted to study a collection of short stories, or an individual story, on your own. This may supplement work done in the class.

- You will need to read each story you are studying several times. Start by reading the story quickly for pleasure, then again slowly and carefully. Further readings will generate new ideas and help you to memorise the details of the story.
- Make careful notes on the themes, plots and characters you come across. Can you spot any themes which occur in more than one story?
- How is the story told? Is it narrated by one of the characters or by an all-seeing (omniscient) narrator who sees into the minds and motives of these imaginary beings?
- Which characters do you like or dislike? Why?
- A short story is different to a novel in lots of ways other than its length. Consider why the author might have chosen to use this method of writing, and how else it differs from other genres.
- Short stories need to have a strong beginning and end to contain the central idea or event. Which stories do this particularly well? Do you like or dislike any particular beginnings or endings?
- Some of the stories are very long, whilst some are very short indeed. Do you think that authors consider the length of their story to be important? What would be gained or lost from making them longer or shorter?

Studying on your own requires self-discipline and a carefully thought-out work plan in order to be effective. Good luck.

Diversity of concerns

The stories in this anthology were all written at some point between the 1830s and the turn of the century. In spite of them sharing a century, there are marked differences in style, cultural background, literary tradition and social setting which make this collection rich in a variety of concerns and viewpoints, and worthy of study for what the student can learn of the century from them.

The authors come from diverse cultural backgrounds: England, America, France, Russia, and South Africa. Therefore, it is interesting to note differences in the way these writers adapt the genre of the short story to their own particular style. In particular, there is a definite contrast of style between the American and English stories.

Literary traditions

There is also a diversity of literary tradition; some authors, such as Charles Dickens, Thomas Hardy, Elizabeth Gaskell, Guy de Maupassant and H.G. Wells, are celebrated novelists and achieved acclaim in their own lifetime, which was not always the case for writers in this period. Some authors, however, came from a journalistic background, and wrote for newspapers and magazines. The rise of the periodical nature of publishing will be covered in detail later in The Historical Perspective of the Story below. These writers tend to date from later in the century, as the popularity of the form and increased proliferation of reading-matter made their work more accessible to the general reader.

Social issues

The wide range of social backgrounds and political concerns echoes popular concern for social issues in this period, and makes study of the anthology within its wider context (see Literary Terms) so interesting. Maupassant highlights discontent over inequalities of wealth in rural France in his story *Country Living*.

Y

Maxim Gorky discusses the same issue in *Twenty-six Men and a Girl*, this time set in pre-Revolutionary Russia. Mrs Gaskell shows the same concerns in the England of the 1840s in *The Half Brothers*. Therefore, despite these cultural and geographical barriers, writers were expressing the same concerns, and showing the same interest in political and social discontent.

Settings

The setting of the stories is equally diverse, spanning the poverty-stricken rural areas of France, the heavily industrialised urban areas of Russia, high-society New York, and the plains of mid-Western America. Each story contains its own special setting, and it is fascinating to compare and contrast these in order to gain wider insight into the times, and also each writer's particular perspective. Setting is an essential part of any work of fiction, and must be viewed as such. For example, Sherlock Holmes is closely identified with London, and he needs to be a gentleman; the stories would not work if he was removed from his cultural and social setting. Similarly, it is essential to the plot of *Lou, the Prophet* that Lou is a foreign settler in America, as it adds to his feelings of isolation and loneliness, which are the reasons for his religious conversion. Characters in short stories are closely linked to their setting. Consider the effect on the story if *Twenty-six Men and a Girl* had been set in more affluent conditions, or if Van Bibber had not been a gentleman. The most essential features of each story would be radically altered if the setting were changed.

Individuals are greatly influenced by their environment. This applies to real life as well as fiction.

Each story is a defined unit in itself, and can be enjoyed on its own. However, there are patterns and links between them – historical, cultural and social – which make them interesting to study as a group.

PART TWO

SUMMARIES

DETAILED SUMMARIES

KATE CHOPIN

The Unexpected

On the surface this story appears to be very brief and matter-of-fact, an unremarkable little tale. However, it would have shocked its readers in 1895, as it deals with issues of physical desire and female emancipation.

Randall and Dorothea are engaged to be married. They clearly are desperately in love with each other, as their separation at the beginning of the story describes the 'bitter' parting as 'too cruel an ordeal to bear'. They write to each other daily for the first month of Randall's absence. Dorothea spends tortured hours alone, reading and rereading his every letter until the paper itself begins to disintegrate.

Note how the descriptive language of Dorothea and her environment contrast with that of Randall.

Towards the end of his business trip, Randall contracts some kind of unspecified illness which prolongs his time away from home. Dorothea is devastated by the news that she will have much longer to wait before being with her fiancé again; and comes to 'the limit of her endurance'. Her parents disapprove of her going to

join her lover, so she has to wait until he is well enough
to travel home to her.

The imagery of Doctors suggest a trip to warmer climes, and Randall is
sickness and able to stop off on his journey to see his beloved. She
weakness is set waits eagerly for him, only to be appalled by the
against the change, both physical and emotional. He is wasted,
powerful language easily exhausted, drawn and fragile in appearance. All
of life and energy. the passion in her description (see Literary Terms) of
him previously fades with her confrontation of this
shadow of the former man. His suggestion to move
forward the marriage date is greeted with repugnance
by her; she draws away from him in abhorrence.

He finally leaves, and she escapes into the country,
pronouncing to herself that she will never marry him, in
spite of his great wealth.

COMMENT   The story appears to be dealing with the dilemma of
being torn between physical and emotional love; what
Dorothea initially mistakes for love is in fact desire.
When she recognises that she no longer desires
Randall, all thoughts of marriage immediately leave her.

Dorothea is clearly not an independent woman; her
family have some control over her life, and a partial
reason for her engagement to Randall is his obvious
wealth. However, in spite of her lack of control, she
makes decisions for herself and shows herself to be
strong and liberated.

The language of the story deals very much with the
sensual aspects of love, which would have caused
something of a sensation when it was published,
especially since it is the woman described as having
these feelings of longing.

The title of the story refers to Dorothea's unexpected
change in plans; it could also highlight the unexpected
way in which she takes matters into her own hands.

TOGETHERNESS?

GLOSSARY   physician doctor

lambent soft, radiant with the sun

THOMAS HARDY

Tony Kytes,
the Arch-
Deceiver

This tale, part of a collection called *Life's Little Ironies*, deals with the themes (see Literary Terms) of love, marriage and honour in the late 1800s. The eponymous (see Literary Terms) hero, clearly a charmer and wooer of women, has lately become engaged to a sweet, innocent girl in his locality, Milly Richards.

The description of
Tony is less than
flattering, yet he is
clearly popular
with women. Do
you think the
narrator (see
Literary Terms)
approves of him?

Unfortunately, Tony does not appear totally sure of his choice. During the course of a wagon ride, he comes across two of his former sweethearts; his renewed contemplation of both proves most disconcerting to him, and he begins to doubt the marital bargain he has made.

Tony's situation grows more and more uncomfortable as he is forced to hide his fiancée and one of his ex-lovers in the back of the cart, to make way for the third, Hannah Jolliver. Just as he is beginning to despair of being able to extricate himself from this very confused state of affairs, he sees his father and stops the cart in order to beg some advice.

Tony's father has one piece of advice to offer; he maintains that his son should marry 'Whichever of 'em did *not* ask to ride with thee' (p. 19). He clearly feels that assertive women are not marriageable propositions.

However, the awkwardness resolves itself without any assistance, for when all three discover that the object of their affections has been making similar declarations of love to all of them, they are of course horrified. Unity and Hannah refuse to have anything more to do with him, but Milly, although devastated by the thought of her sweetheart's apparent lack of devotion, agrees to be his wife.

COMMENT   We learn from the title that the eponymous (see
           Literary Terms) hero has a reputation for philandering,
           and thus there is a powerful sense overriding the story
           that he needs to be taught a lesson.

           Milly is clearly supposed to be the heroine of the story;
           she is described in glowing terms and behaves in a very
           'ladylike' fashion. However, at the end of the story she
           is the third choice, and agrees to marry Tony even after
Consider the form   being totally humiliated by him. This raises questions
her humiliation   about whether in fact we should have any respect for
takes, and whether   her.
you feel she makes   Tony's father does not appear to blame his son totally
the right decision. for getting into this silly situation; in fact it is the two
           women, Hannah and Unity, of whom he clearly
           disapproves. This demonstrates how assertive, free-
           thinking women were frowned upon by this society.

GLOSSARY   **smallpox** contagious viral disease, with fever and pustules
               which usually leave permanent scars
           banns notification through local church of a forthcoming
               marriage
           nunny-watch dialect term meaning pickle, predicament
           miff fuss
           swound faint, swoon

A RNOLD BENNETT

News of the   Arnold Bennett's warm, unassuming story of a son
Engagement   returning home to break the news of his engagement to
           his widowed mother, in fact, highlights some
           interesting ideas about the role of women in that
           society. There is a sense of autobiography in the tone,
           which is influenced by the first-person narration as well
           as the links to the author's own circumstances.

           The narrator (see Literary Terms) is returning home to
           spend Christmas with his mother; two days previously
           he has become engaged to a young lady, and wishes to

TOGETHERNESS?

We receive clues that the narrator's interpretation of events may be flawed, because although we view events from his viewpoint, we are not part of the immediate story, and thus have an overall picture not shared by the narrator.

break this news to his mother. He is extremely preoccupied with the forthcoming announcement, and therefore little suspects that his mother has an announcement of her own to make.

As soon as he arrives, he notices that his mother, whom he describes as 'little and plump', is acting slightly out of character; however, he is so intent upon his own business that he believes her to have hatched a far-fetched plot to invite his fiancée to surprise him, and that this is the cause of the flushed cheeks, bright eyes and animated interest in knocks at the front door.

When he discovers that Mr Nixon, an old friend of the family, has also been invited for supper, he is a little put out; he clearly wants to have his mother to himself so he can tell her his news in private. When it transpires that it is his mother and Mr Nixon who have a similar announcement to make to him, he is very surprised indeed. However, he speedily realises how selfishly he has behaved, how self-immersed, and ends his tale by claiming that 'you live and learn'.

COMMENT

The narrator clearly perceives the irony (see Literary Terms) of the situation in the way he responds to the news of his mother's engagement.

Bennett's character has clearly never paid much attention to his mother; this shows in the way that he makes erroneous assumptions about her. Even his descriptions of her are flat and without substance, highlighting his tendency to take her for granted. He appreciates her as a housewife and social manager, but appears to spend little time considering either her true nature or her own needs.

Their relationship appears to have been dominated by the needs of the son, and although the mother has been a widow for twenty years, he has taken little account of her needing a life of her own. In fact, when noticing her youthful appearance, he describes this as 'remarkable'; communicating his former lack of awareness.

Luckily, he recognises his behaviour as selfish; however, he comments that it is also, although not excusable, very characteristic of the behaviour of a son. Therefore Bennett is displaying a common tendency in the way sole, or eldest, sons are treated by their mothers.

His strong attention to detail and concentration upon the lives of ordinary people and their concerns, displayed effectively in this story, is interesting from a cultural point of view. His style gives readers an effective insight into the preoccupations of his time.

GLOSSARY   **Five Towns** the five 'pottery' towns which surround Stoke-on-Trent
             kittle cattle ticklish, difficult to deal with
             incandescent glowing, shining brightly

E LIZABETH GASKELL

The Half   This story is a typical example of the themes (see
Brothers   Literary Terms) which Mrs Gaskell explored in her
                writing. Although often criticised for its sentimental,
                perhaps melodramatic ending, it shows her deep-felt
                concerns for the issues of duty and morality; also the
                benefits of a pragmatic approach to the difficulties of
                Victorian life amongst the working classes. Much of her
                interest was concentrated upon the harsh working and
                living conditions of the urban factory workers; however,
                this tale is centred around rural, farming people.
                Nevertheless, the issues are similar.

The narrator (see Literary Terms) is one of the two brothers referred to in the title. His mother was married young, and had only been married for three years when her young husband died, leaving her with a baby girl, a failing farm to manage, and pregnant with another child. Her sister comes to live with her and to help out with the child and the imminent birth of the new baby. Soon after the death of her husband, her little girl becomes ill with scarlet fever – a very common disease at that time – and dies. The mother is distraught, but cannot show the emotion she is feeling; only when she has given birth to her son does she let out all her pain and grief. She dotes on the new baby, giving him all the love she feels for both her children; the dead one and the living. She names her son Gregory.

With no Welfare State the family are in danger of starving.

The sisters carry on struggling to manage. They take in 'piece work', sewing for the large factories in the nearby city. Unfortunately, the mother's eyesight begins to fail which makes her incapable of this occupation. The situation is very precarious; rendered more so for the fact that Gregory is not a strong, thriving baby, but needs lots of love and attention.

It is at this point that the mother receives a proposal of marriage from a wealthy neighbouring farmer: a bachelor in his forties named William Preston. The mother, far from being overjoyed at this attention, is highly distressed; however, she makes a pragmatic decision and marries him in order that she and her son will be provided for.

The marriage proves not to be successful. The mother pours all her love and attention on to her son Gregory, and her husband becomes resentful of this. He blames the boy for the fact that his wife does not love him. Their arguments grow, chiefly centred around Gregory. One particularly distressing quarrel causes the mother, who is pregnant with Preston's child, to go into labour early; she sickens and dies, having given birth to the narrator of the story – Gregory's 'half brother'.

William Preston now believes he has further cause to hate Gregory. He blames the boy for causing the death of his wife. The new baby gets all the love, attention

Note echoes of Emily Brontë's Wuthering Heights in the abused, unaccepted relation living a harsh farm life.

and praise meant for both sons. They grow up in very different circumstances – Gregory is tormented, victimised, bullied by Preston and all around him. This turns him into a sulky, loutish youth, apparently dull and stupid. His brother, on the other hand, has all the advantages which can be bought. He receives a good education, and develops a selfish and superior attitude from being used to being the centre of attention.

What may lie behind the smile on Gregory's face when the two brothers are found?

One night, whilst returning home, he gets lost on the Fells. Snow begins to fall, and just at the moment when he is despairing of ever being found, he hears the barking of Lassie, Gregory's dog. His brother has come to look for him. They send the dog back to the farm with a handkerchief around its neck as a message. Gregory covers his brother with all the warm clothes from his own body, and the two shelter together to await help. Unfortunately, help is too long in coming for Gregory, who dies from the cold.

When it is discovered that Gregory laid down his life in order to protect his younger brother, all around feel remorse; especially William Preston, who is haunted by the boy's memory until his own death. The narrator remembers Gregory telling him how their mother entrusted the child to his care: 'Thou canst not remember, lad, how we lay together thus by our dying mother. She put thy small, wee hand in mine – I reckon she sees us now' (p. 42).

COMMENT

This story has a strong religious moral; Gregory displays the Christian doctrine of suffering for those he loves, bearing harsh treatment without complaint, and self-sacrifice. It would be vital for the success of the story, at that time, for the characters to learn from their mistakes and regret their behaviour. The Victorian audience were strongly approving of texts which displayed errant characters mending their ways, or being punished severely. This is a theme (see Literary Terms) of which Dickens was particularly fond. (See Part Three: Commentary.)

It is worth considering what qualities the other main characters represent.

None of the characters are very well developed, and should be perceived more for what values and personality traits they represent; i.e., the narrator (see Literary Terms) is the selfish, spoiled young man who learns humility from the sacrifice of others.

The melodramatic language would appeal to a contemporary audience. Lengthy expressions of emotion, dwelling upon characters' feelings and inner torment, were characteristic of the genre. Mrs Gaskell's use of dialect (see Literary Terms) reflects her interest in the affairs of ordinary people. Death is the most significant feature in the story, occurring no less than five times. The descriptions (see Literary Terms) of funerals, death-bed scenes, and heightened emotional outpourings, are all typical of Mrs Gaskell's writing. The theme (see Literary Terms) of solid, moral people struggling for survival in hard times is again a common idea in fiction of this time; as is the philosophical attitude towards infant mortality and fatal diseases.

GLOSSARY

Consumption tuberculosis, or TB (disease of the lungs, very common in Victorian times)

marring spoiling, damaging

scouted rejected, ridiculed, scorned

fells large stretch of high moor land

gait path, direction

whirl giddy, confused sensation of thoughts

A Identify the speaker.

1 'Never! not for all his thousands! Never, never! not for millions!'

4 'The snow blinds me, and I am feared that in moving about just now, I have lost the right gait homewards'

2 'All three are in that wagon, and what to do with 'em I know no more than the dead'

3 I said nothing about my own engagement that night. I had never thought of my mother as a woman with a future

Identify the person 'to whom' this comment refers.

5 He used to turn silent and quiet – sullen and sulky, my father thought it; stupid, aunt Fanny used to call it. But every one said he was stupid and dull, and this stupidity and dullness grew upon him.

6 'Twas a little, round, firm, tight face, with a seam here and there left by the smallpox, but not enough to hurt his looks in a woman's eye

Check your answers on page 86.

B Consider these issues.

a How each story begins and how it engages the reader's interest.

b The ways in which the author influences opinion of each central character.

c Which of the characters are sympathetic, and how this is achieved.

d Whether the emotionally charged ending of *The Half Brothers* helps your understanding of the story.

e The 'narrative stance' or voice telling the story; is it someone involved in the action or an 'omniscient' narrator? Think what differences are created by using different techniques.

GUY DE MAUPASSANT

Country
Living

Note how the
description of
Madame
d'Hubières is
unflattering. Both
she and Madame
Tuvache do not
escape the author's
critical eye.

The Vallins and the Tuvaches are two peasant families living in rural France. They are very good friends, and their children spend many hours together. Each family has four children under the age of six, and all eight play together all day. Times are very hard, and there is little to eat other than potato water, cabbage and bread. In spite of their financial difficulties, both families appear to survive reasonably well, and seem to get a sense of pride from being able to do so. They work very hard, long hours, and there is no real possibility of things ever improving.

Into this pastoral idyll comes a chance of monetary gain in the shape of Monsieur and Madame Henri d'Hubières. This local couple, clearly greatly financially advantaged, come upon the children one afternoon whilst on a drive. Madame is very much taken with the Tuvaches' youngest child, a little boy. She begins to make regular visits, plying all children with delicacies the like of which they would never have seen.

On one of these visits, the couple approach the Tuvaches and present them with a request: for their youngest child. They offer great financial incentives if the family will allow them to adopt their little boy. He is to have every advantage, to be raised as a gentleman, and to be presented with a very large sum when he comes of age.

Madame Tuvache is horrified by this request. She shows her outrage by demanding that the couple leave immediately; which they do, only to make the same request of the Vallins next door. This time, they meet with more success, and the baby Jean Vallin is carried away by Madame d'Hubières.

Several years pass. Madame Tuvache becomes well
known in the locality as the woman who would not sell
her child; she is upheld as a model of virtue and sound
All has turned out moral sense. She bitterly criticises the Vallins for their
well for the Vallins. actions; they, however, are managing quite nicely on the
Consider why pension bestowed upon them by their benefactors, and
Madame Tuvache appear not to care. One day, the young Jean Vallin,
might appear so now come of age, is brought by Madame d'Hubières to
bitter. visit his parents. There is much celebration at the sight
of the young gentleman, smartly dressed and well
educated, who greets his parents tenderly.

Unfortunately, this is all witnessed by the Tuvaches' son
Charlot – the first choice. When he perceives all he
could have been and had in the shape of his neighbour's
child, he is furious with his parents, criticising their
values and vowing never to see them again. His parents
are devastated.

COMMENT   This story deals head-on with the extreme levels of
wealth and poverty in France at this time. Maupassant
offers a detached, realistic view of what he saw; the
story is undramatic and unbiased, dealing rather in a
matter-of-fact manner with the events.

The peasant families are faced with an extremely
uncomfortable moral dilemma: how best to serve the
needs of their child. Madame Tuvache takes the
emotional view, seeing her duty as providing for all her
children herself, although that may mean a struggle for
all of them. The Vallins, on the other hand, take the
pragmatic approach; by doing so they give their
youngest child a great opportunity whilst making their
own lives more comfortable into the bargain. Things
work out well for them; their son returns, and feels
nothing but gratitude to his sensible parents.

Madame Tuvache gets her satisfaction in the
intervening years for having made the more honourable

choice, and yet is left at the end with her son's fury that she did not act differently. The ironic (see Literary Terms) twist raises questions about what constitutes good parenting, as well as making a discreet comment on the moral values of the peasantry as Maupassant saw them. Although he takes the stance of impartial observer, there is a hint of unease in his treatment of Madame Tuvache. Is she clinging on to her moral ideology because there is little else to cling to?

GLOSSARY   **rancid** stale fat, putrid

                   sententiously speaking pompously, high-handedly

RICHARD HARDING DAVIS

Van Bibber's Burglar

Courtland Van Bibber, the gentleman hero of many of Richard Harding Davis's stories, appears here in a tale very popular in its day. Van Bibber mirrors many of the qualities for which Davis was renowned, and has been seen as an idealised emulation of the author's most notorious qualities. As gentleman lover, rich man-about-town, Van Bibber encounters several adventures

in his own collection of stories. This tale, whilst being interesting in terms of highlighting American late nineteenth-century attitudes towards the social divide, as seen from the big city perspective, also has a darker edge of social commentary to it which makes it particularly worthy of study.

Van Bibber and his friend Travers, two well-to-do young gentlemen of New York, are spending an evening out together. Having been to a dance in quest of a young lady who is clearly the latest love in Van Bibber's life, they then go to a boxing match. They are patently stepping into a world unfamiliar to them, and go to great pains to disguise their obvious social standing and superior public position.

Notice how one of the reporters describes city life as repetitive and mundane, yet both Van Bibber and his burglar prove that people can act unpredictably.

When the fight is over, they, together with some journalists from the match, go to eat at an all-night restaurant. During the evening they discuss the merits of big-city life, the journalists commenting that it is in fact very mundane and unromantic, the only potentially interesting events inevitably materialising as 'vulgar' and sordid. Several famous novelists of the day are mentioned as having partaken of the New York experience, amongst them great social commentators such as Dickens, Balzac and R.L. Stevenson. Intent on their conversation, they are only vaguely aware that a beggar woman and a group of unruly citizens have to be shepherded from the premises by the restaurant owner.

The party disband at dawn, and Van Bibber begins to make his way home, accompanied by the first milk carts. On a deserted stretch of road he notices a face appear from a passageway door; he is suspicious of the man's obvious unease and decides to investigate. When he discovers that he is clearly a burglar, he confronts him with a great show of bravado and disarms him.

The burglar tells Van Bibber hopelessly of his plight. A newly released convict, he is desperate to rejoin his family but cannot raise money for the fare. Van Bibber takes pity on the man, and after returning the stolen belongings, he takes him to the station and pays his fare to Montana. After the train has departed, Van Bibber reads in the newspaper the news that a notorious burglar, ironically (see Literary Terms) nicknamed 'Jimmie the Gent', has been helped to escape from a local jail and is presumably in New York. Van Bibber views this piece of news sagaciously, in full knowledge that the story is parallel to his own recent experience.

COMMENT

See whether there are any other points in the story that show Van Bibber to have a kind nature.

Van Bibber is not at ease with this kind of moral dilemma; his life is geared towards gentlemanly pursuits generally, and he has the air of one who does not have to work for a living. In spite of this, his character is neither shallow or trivial; he recognises a genuine dilemma and acts according to his moral conscience rather than his societal one. This is highlighted strongly when he and the burglar walk past a policeman and his feelings of guilt are assuaged by the thought of 'the wife and child who lived in the West', and who were 'straight'.

He enters a world which he has not inhabited before, and is forced to confront the difficulties faced by those less advantaged than himself and his peers. The comment is made that some of the great authors who have visited New York have been more aware of the social divide than New York residents themselves; the observation made by Dickens is particularly significant.

There are two possible interpretations of the end of the story; either Van Bibber's burglar is in fact 'Jimmie the Gent', which would mean Van Bibber has been naïvely duped, or the story in the paper is about another burglar entirely, in which case there are strong parallels to his own actions in the manner in which Jimmie's friends assisted his escape. Either way it appears irrelevant to Van Bibber, who is conscious that he has acted according to his own conscience, with a slightly

Y

ironic (see Literary Terms) self-consciousness of his reputation as a gentleman and an adventurer. In the closing lines he settles comfortably back into his own world. He acts according to his sense of personal morality, taking responsibility for one tiny element of social injustice rather than rising above and remaining aloof as his contemporaries appear to do.

GLOSSARY   **Philistine** uncultured, commonplace person

hack driver driver of a horse-drawn hackney carriage

Turkish bath equivalent to modern-day sauna, used as a social meeting-place frequented by gentlemen

the Society presumably a group who worked to reestablish offenders into the community

OSCAR WILDE

The Nightingale and the Rose

In typical fairy tale (see Literary Terms) fashion, the characters in this short story by Oscar Wilde need to be perceived as what they represent rather than who they are. First published in 1888 as part of a collection for children called *The Happy Prince and Other Stories*, it has survived 100 years of changing tastes and attitudes. One possible reason for this is the differing levels on which the story can be interpreted; it certainly stands in its own right as a tale for children, but appeals to an adult audience in its implicit comments on the nature of art and love.

She is devoted to him; it is interesting to consider whether he is worthy of her devotion.

The Nightingale lives in an oak tree in the garden of the Student. She dedicates her life to singing sweetly for the benefit of others. One day she overhears the Student, who is distraught because the girl he loves will only dance with him at the ball if he presents her with a red rose, and there are none to be found. The Nightingale is very moved by this, for she feels she recognises true love in the Student's heart. She sets out to assist him in his quest for a red rose.

She travels through the garden, searching and making enquiries. Other dwellers of the garden notice the distress of the Student, but do not share Nightingale's sympathy for his suffering. Green Lizard mocks the very idea of crying for the lack of a red rose.

Eventually she comes to the rose bush which will supply her with a single red rose, but her part of the bargain is very severe. She must sing to the bush all night long, and allow one of its thorns to pierce her heart. The Nightingale agrees, believing that she is sacrificing herself for love, which is greater than life, and for the heart of a man, which is greater than that of a bird.

Her plan comes to fruition; the next morning Nightingale's lifeless body is found at the foot of a bush bearing a single, perfect red rose. The Student rushes off ecstatically to his love, only to be scornfully rejected in favour of a wealthier suitor. The rose is thrown carelessly into the street, and the Student decides to take up philosophy.

COMMENT

The student does not recognise pure art in the Nightingale's voice; he misunderstands her and plainly is not worthy of her song.

This is a very poignant story; the sacrifice of the Nightingale is heightened in intensity by the obvious lack of worth on the part of the Student and his love. The bird's actions could be seen as wasted, because they are not appreciated by those to whom they were directly meant to benefit. In spite of this, the Nightingale's selfless action stands alone as something pure and perfect, like the rose she created.

The Nightingale is perceived as standing directly in opposition to the Student, who is not really as much in love as he thinks he is. He is merely toying with the role of hopeless romantic, whereas the bird represents the true nature of romance. Both he and the woman disregard true love, she preferring financial gain and he turning to study, whereas the Nightingale sacrifices herself for the one thing she believes in above all others.

The fairy-tale quality is created by the technique of personification; animals and plants communicate by the spoken tongue. This technique enables the story to work on more than one level. Many fairy tales function in this way: communicating more than one level of meaning. Think how stories such as *Red Riding Hood*, whilst being on the one hand children's entertainment, also serve as a moral lesson and a warning of the consequences of bad behaviour.

Wilde is making a comment on his perception of the role of the artist in society: to sacrifice oneself for one's art in order that others may have pleasure. We see this in the Nightingale's willingness to sacrifice herself for the Student although he does not appreciate or understand her at all.

GLOSSARY   **Pomegranate** exotic fruit, full of pips (see story of Persephone in Greek mythology)

Echo again from Greek mythology: the young girl Echo was punished for her insolence by being made to spend her life repeating back whatever was said to her. She was so ashamed that she ran away to the hills to spend her life in cavernous places

EST YOURSELF (Section II)

  Identify the speaker.

1 'It's a thing nobody's got no right asking a mother to do. I won't have it! It'd be sinful and wicked!'

5 'Yet Love is better than Life, and what is the heart of a bird compared to the heart of a man?'

2 'Parents like you is the reason why children get held back'

3 'You're a pretty poor sort of burglar, I should say'

4 'No red rose in all my garden'

Identify the person 'to whom' this comment refers.

6 ''Twas a tempting offer, right enough. But she wasn't interested. She done what a good mother oughter'

7 He felt very guilty as he passed each policeman, but he recovered himself when he thought of the wife and child who lived in the West, and who were 'straight'

Check your answers on page 86.

 Consider these issues.

a How Oscar Wilde manages to write a story that will have equal appeal to adults and children. Are there any other stories in the collection which communicate on more than one level?

b The similarities and differences between the characters of Van Bibber and Sherlock Holmes.

c The translation of *Country Living* into English; how does the written dialect (see Literary Terms) affect your understanding of the story?

d To what extent you feel sympathy for the actions of the Nightingale.

e Whether you feel Van Bibber did the right thing by helping the burglar to escape.

OLIVE SCHREINER

The Woman's Rose

Olive Schreiner was a fiercely political woman. Her childhood in South Africa was shadowed by severe racial tension; her parents were ardently religious, and she grew up surrounded by extreme poverty and extremely strict household rules. These experiences contributed to her later pacifism and feminism. *The Woman's Rose* highlights her particular regard for the importance of female solidarity and loyalty.

The narrator (see Literary Terms) introduces this story by going through the contents of a 'memory' box, and coming to the item of central importance: a white rose. Other flowers (from male suitors) have been kept for a while but eventually discarded, but this single rose has remained. She recounts the circumstances by which she came by this rose.

This suggests that the value of a woman's friendship (symbolised in the gift of a rose) is more enduring than that of a man.

As a young girl of fifteen she was visiting a small, new town, largely inhabited by men – possibly a town set up to accommodate mine workers. Of the very few women residing there, there is one who commands immense attention and praise from the men. They continually send her flowers and other presents, call upon her, take her riding, even propose. She appears to respond with dignity to these attentions, but favours no man in particular. She reigns supreme as most admired female in the town.

When the narrator of the story arrives, the situation changes. Because she is a fresh face to gaze upon, a novelty, all eyes turn to her. The first lady is forgotten and overlooked in the desire to pour all the attention upon the visitor. She is flattered by all the attention, but is far more concerned with the feelings of the other woman. Apart from admiring her beauty, she also desperately wants to be friends with her, and is distressed by the thought that the woman probably hates her for taking away all the attention.

The night before she is due to end her visit, she attends a dance. The other woman is there, wearing a single white rose – the only one available for miles, a gift from an admirer. Whilst they are preparing to enter the dance, the woman suddenly takes the rose and bestows it upon her adversary: a gift of friendship from one woman to another. The narrator looks back upon this event, and its significance raises her spirits whenever she remembers the rose.

COMMENT   There is more of the anecdotal (see Literary Terms) than narrative in this tale; the theme (see Literary Terms) is far more important than the story or characters. In fact the story is merely a device by which to highlight the importance of female friendship and loyalty. No names are mentioned, or details of personality. The characters have the substance of shadows.

Many women kept such boxes, with significant personal effects, such as letters and mementoes.

She describes the box as a container for trifles, thus minimising and trivialising the value of what is kept inside. The rose, however, does not have purely personal significance. To the narrator (see Literary Terms), this gift of a rose is far more important than any of the attentions she receives from male suitors. It is symbolic of the special value of female friendship, and she keeps the knowledge of it as a talisman to remind her of the strength and importance of women in a society dominated by male doctrines and power.

The story is interesting to observe in terms of the social and political climate of the time. The Suffrage movement was in its infancy, and women did not have the vote until some twenty years after it was written. Therefore the author's political activism is evident in that she was campaigning for such ideas before society was generally aware of them.

GLOSSARY   Colonial inhabitant of British colony in colonised country such
                  as America or India; referring here to South Africa
                  magnanimity generosity, thoughtfulness

C HARLOTTE PERKINS GILMAN

The Yellow   This strange, vaguely supernatural tale traces the events
Wallpaper   and circumstances leading to the nervous breakdown of
                      a Victorian, middle-class wife. Largely
                      autobiographical, it touches on many of the social and
                      political issues close to the heart of its author.

                      The narrator (see Literary Terms) of the story and her
                      husband, a doctor, have rented a large country mansion
                      for three months of the summer. The wife writes the
                      diary entries which form this story; therefore rather
                      than being viewed from the perspective of hindsight, we
                      feel drawn closer to her experience by being privy to her
                      thoughts and feelings as they occur: 'this is dead paper
                      and a great relief to my mind' (p. 79).

Her illness is not   The narrator (we never know her name) is supposedly
referred to   suffering from some kind of undefined illness, which is
specifically, which the reason for the country retreat. She believes herself
shows Victorian   to be suffering from a real complaint, but all around her
concern to keep   apparently agree with her husband, the doctor, that
such matters   there is nothing wrong other than a 'temporary nervous
covered and   depression'. She has been forbidden to 'work' (her own
private.   inverted commas, which imply that those close to her
                      do not view her writing as real, or important, and
                      merely humour her).

                      Our heroine disagrees with these opinions, and covertly
                      rebels against them. One form of resistance comes from
                      her refusal to stop writing in her diary. Another is in
                      her comments themselves, by which we perceive that
                      she dislikes some of the strictures which have been
                      placed about her, even though she trustingly believes
                      they have been enforced out of love and care.

As the story slowly unfolds, the narrator gives more information about the house, and the bedroom which she dislikes intensely. She describes the large, airy 'nursery' in which she and her husband sleep. This room, we are told, has bars to the windows, rings embedded in the walls, and large areas of the hated wallpaper torn away. She assumes the reason for all these is to do with the room once being 'a nursery, then a playroom, then a gymnasium'; however there is a sense of foreboding, a hint that these changes to the room may not have such a simple explanation as she believes.

The story picks up again at irregular intervals, whenever she has time alone to write. Therefore we are drawn to empathise (see Literary Terms) with her feelings of empty time, loneliness and boredom. She spends more and more hours at home alone; her husband is away for long intervals, and she is left in the care of her sister-in-law. We discover there is a baby son, with which she appears to have little to do, although she refers to him very fondly: 'such a dear baby! And yet I cannot be with him, it makes me so nervous' (p. 82).

Notice how the entrance of the husband into the bedroom allows us to see another's reaction to her behaviour, and clarify our understanding of reality.

She draws more and more into herself, spending the large part of the day alone in the room with the yellow wallpaper. Her fascination with it grows; she follows the patterns it makes, spending hours tracing the irregular design. As she keeps more and more to herself, so she gets more entranced by the wallpaper, which begins to obsess her. She begins to make out 'a strange, provoking, formless sort of figure that seems to skulk about behind that silly and conspicuous front design'. Her obsession with this figure grows, reaching a startling climax whereby she has descended into madness, actually 'becoming' the figure she perceived behind the wallpaper. It is only when we see her husband's reaction to her behaviour that we can appreciate the strangeness of it, being able to see it objectively rather than from the perspective of the narrator.

COMMENT   This story can be read on different levels; it has appeared in anthologies of ghost stories, and will comfortably fit into that genre. However, it is also commenting upon Victorian attitudes towards women, particularly in this case towards those who wish to pursue a professional interest in 'The Arts' (see Part Three: Commentary).

Because the narrator (see Literary Terms) is the central character, the audience perceives events entirely from her point of view. This can distort our impression of reality. It can also be a significant indicator of the narrator's state of mind.

GLOSSARY   **Phosphates or phosphites** effervescent drink, taken for medicinal reasons; largely ineffective

piazza veranda of house, overlooking garden

arbor area of garden shaded by trees

Romanesque style of art and architecture in Romanised Europe, particularly 1050–1200

delirium tremens disordered state of mind with tremors and delusions, linked to alcohol abuse.

MAXIM GORKY

Twenty-six Men and a Girl   This story, bitter and sombre in tone, recounts Gorky's own personal experience of working in a bakery. He writes with a strong sense of realism, preferring this to the romantic idealism of some of his contemporaries. A committed Socialist, Gorky dwelled at length upon the themes (see Literary Terms) of social injustice, the nature of humanity, and the fight between the best and the worst in human nature when placed under difficult conditions.

The narrator (see Literary Terms) who recounts this story in the first person, is one of twenty-six 'convicts' living a life of virtual slavery in nineteenth-century Russia. They are referred to as prisoners and yet it is never made clear whether their lives are, in fact, some kind of punishment for an undefined crime. This in itself makes the point that their living conditions are terrible; they are suffering the same abuse as someone convicted of a crime and imprisoned.

Harsh conditions have reduced the men to a semi-trance state of existence; serving a long period of imprisonment de-socialises the inmate.

Working for a baker, they spend their whole lives together in the basement of a bakery, preparing the dough for the tons of pretzels which pass through the bakery on a daily basis. Their lives have become monotonous in the extreme – they no longer look at each other, let alone speak. As the author says: 'There was nothing to talk about and we had become accustomed to the silence, broken only by the sound of cursing, for you can always find a reason to curse someone, especially if he is a mate' (p. 98). They have nothing pleasant or of value in their lives to bring them joy. The occasional bout of mournful singing raises their spirits momentarily; however this is sporadic and brings no real comfort to their impoverished lives. Thus the daily appearance of a young girl, Tanya, takes on a great significance for them.

Does Tanya deserve the glowing terms, the adoration with which she is described?

Tanya works in one of the rooms above the bakery. She is sixteen, pretty and cheerful. Her visits each morning to collect some pretzels from the bakers give them something to look forward to, and thus they invest all their interest in life into the shape of this young girl. They discuss her merits at length, and all appear to care for her deeply, with a protective and idealised love.

The head baker appears to have a more cynical view. He suspects Tanya is not so perfect as his peers believe.

Their employer takes on the services of a young man, handsome and friendly but very conceited. He spends many hours with the bakers, bragging about his exploits with women. The twenty-six, having so little else in their lives, enjoy his company and listen eagerly to his tales; however one of them clearly does not appreciate the man's vanity and lack of respect for women, for he challenges the young man to tempt Tanya in the same manner. Although all twenty-six are appalled at the idea, they are confident of Tanya's virtue and purity, thus are shocked and stunned when, inevitably, she succumbs to his advances. They turn upon her in a bout of vitriolic rage, pouring out all their frustration and anger. The story ends with her turning away from her erstwhile friends for ever: 'And we were left standing in the middle of the yard, in the mud and the rain under the grey, sunless sky' (p. 111).

COMMENT

The first part of the story focuses on the terrible living and working conditions of these men, thereby highlighting their desperate need for anything to bring a ray of interest or distraction into their day.

Both Tanya and the soldier offer a sense of escape for them; both are perceived in very positive lights by the bakers. It is made clear to the reader, however, that both objects of admiration are highly unworthy.

The bakers attack Tanya so viciously because she has let

them down; she manifested the one opportunity to admire something perfect. When they are made to realise their own mistake, it is she who bears the blame for shattering their illusions.

There is a contrast between the bakers' view of Tanya and the readers'. At several points in the story it is clear that their impression of her is clouded by their need to believe in her purity and virtue. Similarly, it is easy for us to see the Soldier in a more realistic light, even though we appreciate how the men value the distraction he offers.

GLOSSARY **pretzel** crisp knot-shaped biscuit flavoured with salt
black bread coarse rye bread

A Identify the speaker.

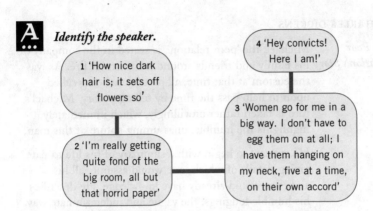

1 'How nice dark hair is; it sets off flowers so'

2 'I'm really getting quite fond of the big room, all but that horrid paper'

3 'Women go for me in a big way. I don't have to egg them on at all; I have them hanging on my neck, five at a time, on their own accord'

4 'Hey convicts! Here I am!'

Identify the person 'to whom' this comment refers.

5 We would rush to open the door for her, jostling each other, and she would come in looking so sweet and happy, holding up her apron, and stand in front of us, her head a little to one side and smiling all the while

6 If she had raised her little finger, I suppose, she might have married any one out of twenty of them

Check your answers on page 86.

B Consider these issues.

a How Maxim Gorky presents the reader with a different perception of Tanya from the one held by the convicts.

b How the narrative structure of *The Yellow Wallpaper* allows the reader to experience events from the narrator's (see Literary Terms) point of view. What does this add to the experience of reading the story?

c The fact that the two women of *The Woman's Rose* barely speak, and yet manage to form a close bond with each other.

d How *The Yellow Wallpaper* easily fits into the category of supernatural tale and political feminist story.

e How all three stories in this section are relayed by the narrative of a central character. What does this contribute to the experience of reading the stories?

CHARLES DICKENS

The Poor Relation's Story Michael, the 'poor relation', is seated in the company of his family and friends around a Christmas fire. As was the custom at that time, all parties are being called upon to help pass the time by telling a story. Michael's turn is taken rather unwillingly, which immediately highlights the humble, unassuming nature of this man.

He appears to begin with a summary of his life to date, giving details of which, one would assume, all his audience would already have knowledge. He describes his humble lodgings, the vague and indeterminate way he spends his days; how he is reliant upon the charity of acquaintances for company, has very little income, and is generally quite a solitary fellow. His only source of unmitigated pleasure comes in the shape of his nephew, Little Frank. This child, we are told, is very similar in habit and character to his uncle, and the latter clearly dotes upon the boy. There are sidelong references to a business partner, an ex-fiancée, and a rather cantankerous old benefactor.

Do you think he is resentful of others for his reduced circumstances? Under the surface of this information, however, there are hints of extreme ill-luck in the past; the business partner having taken advantage of Michael's trusting nature and cheating him in some respect, the fiancée leaving him for another, the uncle disinheriting him. Nevertheless, Michael does not appear to bear any soul ill-will. In fact, he appears to blame himself for his rather lowly circumstances, claiming to be 'nobody's enemy but my own'. He is presented as a victim of circumstances, only to be blamed for a certain naïveté of nature which has allowed others to take advantage of him.

His overall tone of meek acceptance of his fate is rather dramatically cut short when he begins to tell the assembled company that everything he has just claimed,

Is his dignified
stance a true
reflection of his
feelings?

and everything they believe to be true about his life could not be further from the truth. His voice becomes more assured as he begins to paint a strikingly different picture. He returns to the day when he was disinherited by his uncle for wanting to marry his love, Christina. This moment is clearly the pivot for his fall in circumstances, for it is here, we are to understand, where she left him for a rich man. He announces to the company that, in fact, she remained loyal, married him, and they have several children, live in a 'Castle', and that his business partner has not betrayed him but is his closest friend. He describes the contented life that he leads, surrounded by friends and family, love and happiness. It is only when asked where his residence is that we understand, for his reply is 'in the air'.

COMMENT

For the total novice, this story serves as an excellent introduction to the work of Dickens. It contains all the essential elements of a typical Dickensian tale: the list of characters with oddly sounding names, the gentle, meek central figure, the strong moral message. He had great powers of comic and dramatic invention, particularly with regard to character. His fertile humour and biting social criticism created some of the most abhorrent figures in literature. He tended towards caricature (see Literary Terms) rather than in-depth study; his characters were more often symbolic of type rather than fully rounded. He also invested much of his own personal experience in his characters, and in the portrayal of those about whom he himself felt most deeply. Often, however, he could not rise above the sentimental.

He has been described as being the champion of the powerless, and certainly his greatest works are those which contain a mixture of sympathy for the down-trodden and weakest members of society, together with a sharp satirical (see Literary Terms) eye for those in

positions of power. He objected bitterly to the
Victorian British class-system, believing that the
unequal distribution of wealth and power contributed to
the abject misery and poverty suffered by many at that
time. Although a staunch critic, however, he was not a
reformer; he scarcely proffered ideas for practical
change.

The central idea of this story is that of a good, pure but
rather sentimentalised character bearing up bravely
under the cruelty of those surrounding him. This is a
familiar idea in Dickens, and reappears in many guises
throughout his work. Michael invents an alternative
reality for himself as a way of coping with the
emptiness and melancholy of his existence. He does this
as a way of dealing with the disappointment of being
abused by those closest to him.

Consider the
techniques used in
order to
communicate this
information to the
reader.

Although Michael claims that no one is to blame for
his circumstances but himself, the whole picture begins
to make itself plain to the reader from very early on in
his narrative.

Michael's manner of narration alters when he begins to
explain to his audience their mistaken assumptions
about him. His quicker pace, louder tone and more
positive, lively vocabulary all indicate that he is happier
and more confident when concentrating upon his
imaginary world. There is a sense of the man who
might have been, had circumstances been different.

GLOSSARY   **Jezebel** shameless woman (wife of Ahab in Old Testament)
             speculation an investment that incurs risk of a loss
             erroneous mistaken

WILLA CATHER

Lou, the
Prophet

Willa Cather lived among a mainly Danish farming community in Nebraska, one of many pioneering colonies in America in the nineteenth century. She liked and admired the people, and much of her fiction dwelled upon the difficulties faced by these simple, honest farmers. They faced many hardships, not least of which was isolation from their cultural identity. The farming life was barren and back-breaking, many pioneers failing in their attempts to scratch a living from the soil of Mid-Western America.

Lou, a young, second-generation Danish pioneer, has staked his claim and is working very hard to make it pay. However, the summers of Nebraska are long and hard and his crop is in serious danger of failing. Machinery he has bought on the strength of the crop yield is adding further to his financial burden. The young lady promised to him has married another with better prospects and stronger financial returns. He is a simple soul, friendly and kind but not bright. His mother comes regularly to visit him and help out with domestic duties; when she dies, he feels that his lot is very hard to bear indeed. His whole future survival depends on rainfall, which shows no sign of

Consider whether
Lou, driven to
despair, is turning
to God as a last
resort, or does the
author intend us
to believe his
transformation
has occurred
because he has
been chosen by
God?

materialising.

One night he has a very vivid dream: a religious dream. He spends a few days fasting and praying. He appears to have experienced a religious conversion. He goes to his local town where he is greeted by some young boys of the area – friends of his. They become semi-disciples, shielding him from the suspicion of the town, who want him arrested for his uncharacteristic, wild behaviour. The boys hide him in a cave and bring him food, listening avidly to his warnings about the imminent approach of the end of the world.

Eventually, Lou breaks out of his shelter and flees, having experienced another vision. He believes he is going to be taken to Heaven by God; his subsequent disappearance may be interpreted that way, but sceptics believe him to have fallen into quicksand and died. His disciples remain loyal to the end believing him to have been taken by God.

COMMENT   There are strong parallels here with the depiction of the suffering of Jesus at the hands of non-believers. There is even symbolic value in Lou's choice of hiding place.

Lou is clearly a man pushed to the extreme of human suffering. Is it possible that the author is commenting here upon the nature of religious beliefs? Religious sceptics maintain that there is something in every human which craves understanding of the world and assurance of life after death. A sceptical view would see how Lou's conversion comes at a particularly convenient time for him: at the very moment when he cannot take any more, he is given a 'way out' in the form of a religious experience. We are told he is rather dull-witted, which would presumably reinforce the idea of him misunderstanding or placing too great a significance upon his dream.

He is an outsider both in the country and in his own community. His only friends are children. The towns-people distrust him for this, and also because they would be suspicious of the dramatic change in behaviour exhibited by Lou. Nevertheless, their treatment of him appears rather extreme.

GLOSSARY   **plow** US spelling for plough
              sorghum molasses treacle produced from sorghum grass – very primitive food

H. G. WELLS

*The Stolen
Bacillus*

A scientist is showing a visitor around his laboratory. The visitor is a stranger, arriving only with a letter of introduction from an alleged mutual acquaintance. The scientist is a bacteriologist – that is, his work involves studying the bacteria which cause human disease, presumably in an effort to control and subvert the effects of them.

The scientist is clearly enjoying his audience, and being able to enthral his visitor with the details of his work. In an effort to astound him further, he produces a tube which, he informs the visitor, is full of live cholera bacteria. He neglects to notice his guest's odd behaviour: the glint in his eye when he considers the potential effects of such a possession, the 'morbid pleasure' he displays whilst listening to the scientist getting carried away with his description of what devastation would be wreaked by this bacteria being released into the city's water supply.

*All three
characters turn out
to have
questionable
motives for their
actions; consider
how the scientist
explains to his
wife his reasons
for lying to the
thief.*

When the scientist realises that his guest has taken advantage of a moment alone and fled with a stolen phial, he immediately panics and goes in pursuit. An absurd chase ensues; the scientist's wife following her husband and the thief, all three in horse-drawn carriages. The action is related to the reader by London cab-drivers, who comment on the race and lay bets as to its possible outcome.

This story is particularly easy to date as late Victorian by the details, such as concern with cholera poisoning.

When eventually the test tube cracks, the thief drinks the contents and prepares to die, spreading destruction on his way. However, the scientist has realised that the tube, far from containing cholera bacteria, is instead full of a strange virus which turns mammals blue. The thief leaves the scene under the impression that he is spreading death around the population of London, when in fact he has a very strange fate indeed awaiting him.

COMMENT

Cholera, diphtheria, polio and scarlet fever were partially responsible for the high mortality rates in Victorian England, particularly amongst children. It was due to the efforts of scientists that vaccinations were produced to combat the devastating effects of these virulent diseases. Of course, better understanding of hygiene also assisted this process; once the correlation was made between a clean water supply and good sewerage systems and the spread of disease, the mortality rate fell dramatically.

The fear of Anarchy would be real to the Victorians, who valued a sense of order and hierarchy.

The thief claims to be an Anarchist – someone who wishes to upturn the normal order of things and create chaos. However, it is apparent that he is a rather pathetic figure who has gone unnoticed all his life and wishes to become famous through a significant deed. The sense of pathos is compounded by the vision of him walking away from the action, aware of his erroneous assumptions and the rather ludicrous fate which awaits him.

The wife's actions are worthy of comment: her hurry to protect her husband from the condemnation of polite society, by leaving the house in indoor attire, highlights the importance placed upon the rules of etiquette in the middle classes. Her behaviour, together with the cab chase, reduces the second half of the story to the level of a farce. Her notions of duty and subservience seem somewhat uncomfortable to us now, but are interesting to observe from a historical perspective. She has little interest or involvement in his work, and patently is on the periphery of his working life.

Consider how the wife is solely concerned with the social implications of her husband's behaviour, and cannot cope with the seriousness of the situation he has to deal with.

Wells gives the cab-drivers an exaggerated Cockney dialect, which appears to be an indicator of their lowly status, especially when contrasted with the rhetoric of the scientist and political speeches of the thief. Thus they emerge as comic characters, whose only function is to be external commentators to the action rather than being directly involved in its importance.

H.G. Wells is famous for his science fiction (see Literary Terms) writing; there are many elements of this story which have particular relevance today, especially science struggling to understand and control vicious diseases, bacteria used for political reasons, etc. It is worth considering what other elements of this story would not be out of place in our society.

The wife appears to have control over her errant husband at the end of the story; she insists that he must put on his outdoor things in order to present the figure of a gentleman. Ironically (see Literary Terms), he conforms to her wishes in spite of having just been involved with matters of a potentially world-shattering nature.

GLOSSARY **phlegmatic** impassive, unemotional
Teutonic of Germanic origin
Vive l'Anarchie 'Long live Anarchy' – the chant of the French Anarchists in the eighteenth century

EDGAR ALLAN POE

Hop-Frog

Set in an unspecific kingdom, with castles and courtiers, ministers and jesters, *Hop-Frog* would not seem out of place in a book of fairy tales (see Literary Terms). It has a strong moral message, a striking dénouement (see Literary Terms) and a sense of justice such as are found in all good stories for children. However, Edgar Allan Poe was more noted for tales of horror and the supernatural, this story being apparently a favourite with Steven King; even the Brothers Grimm would possibly baulk at having a tale so violent contributing to a collection of theirs.

Hop-Frog is a cripple and a dwarf, enslaved to a cruel and vicious king in a land far away from his home. His only companion is Trippetta, another dwarf, also captive. The pair has been sent as presents to a king who takes pride in having dwarves amongst his courtiers. He treats them both cruelly; they are objects to be used and abused rather than people in their own right. The function of a jester, or fool, at court, would be to have a ready wit and sharp tongue to amuse company at a second's notice; to tell tall tales and jokes, but also to be a laughable figure himself, with some kind of deformity worthy of humorous comment. Hop-Frog fits all criteria, and is also extremely intelligent.

The challenging language, along with the level of assumed knowledge, highlights the extent to which this is a story for adults rather than children.

The king has planned a large masquerade to celebrate a state occasion. As he prides himself on being 'an inimitable joker' along with his seven, equally foul ministers, he wants to create a costume which will not only greatly amuse his guests, but strengthen his reputation as a master of wit. However, on the day of the party itself, he has still come up with no idea. He calls for Hop-Frog to assist.

One of the king's perennial sources of humour with Hop-Frog is to insist he partake of alcohol, knowing that it makes the dwarf very ill. Hop-Frog deals with this treatment resignedly, because he is at the mercy of the king. On this occasion the king is in a particularly cruel frame of mind, and reminds Hop-Frog of all his 'absent friends', which causes tears to come to Hop-Frog's eyes. When the king hits his beloved Trippetta, this is the last straw for the dwarf, and he introduces the king and the seven ministers to his plan for the masquerade: the Eight Chained Ourang-Outangs.

This gruesome plot is typical of Poe's style, where the gory and bloodthirsty are often present.

When all eight are daubed in tar, covered in highly flammable flax, and chained in a circle, they enter the masquerade, causing hysterical outbursts from the assembled guests. The chain is lifted to the high ceiling, whereupon Hop-Frog sets them all alight and escapes through a skylight window with Trippetta. The guests are left below, surveying the carnage. Hop-Frog finally gets his revenge.

COMMENT

Edgar Allan Poe was American, and this story was written during the time of the Abolition of Slavery movement. There are perceivable links here to issues of slavery: people removed against their will from their homeland, reduced to the status of slaves; even the images of chains and monkeys have significance. In true fairy tale style, the events and characters are a metaphor (see Literary Terms) for comments upon the nature of political authority and the corruption of power.

It is a very challenging read, with an uncomfortable ending, although we are glad Hop-Frog gets his revenge. Poe has created a monstrous image in his depiction of the dwarf which challenges our tendency to have pity only for those towards whom we easily feel protective and empathic (see Literary Terms); even though he is treated cruelly, he bears his trouble with fortitude, bravely defends the woman he loves, and overall shows a nobility of nature lacking in the king.

The biting satire (see Literary Terms) of Poe is greatly
in evidence in his depiction of the king, together with
the heavily ironic (see Literary Terms) passages
regarding the king's sense of humour, girth and
wisdom.

GLOSSARY   **Rabelais** sixteenth-century French satirist, noted for his coarse
              humour and language
              Voltaire satirical French writer, part of the Enlightenment
              movement of the eighteenth century; dry and sceptical.
              (Mention of both is ironic (see Literary Terms): to highlight the
              king's ignorance of any writers at all)

Identify the speaker.

1 'Sometimes, one of my relations or acquaintance is so obliging as to ask me to dinner. Those are holiday occasions, and then I generally walk in the Park'

4 'Look at the baby! This is the gentleman who, people say, is nobody's enemy but his own'

3 'Well! I suppose I shall be the first. *Phew!* Anyhow, I shall be a Martyr. That's something. But it is a filthy death, nevertheless. I wonder if it hurts as much as they say'

2 'I have found out why it don't rain, it's because of the sins of the world. You don't know how wicked the world is, it's all bad, even Denmark'

Identify the person 'to whom' this comment refers.

5 'Poor fellow, his large eyes gleamed, rather than shone; for the effect of wine on his excitable brain was not more powerful than instantaneous'

6 A disturbing thought struck him. He turned to the bench by the vapour-bath, and then very quickly to his writing-table. Then he felt hastily in his pockets, and then rushed to the door

Check your answers on page 86.

 Consider these issues.

a The ways the author engages sympathy for Hop-Frog in spite of the grotesque description of him and his violent actions.

b How the cab chase becomes farcical due to the exaggerated 'Cockney' commentary of the cab men.

c How Dickens gives tiny snippets of details about Michael's daily routine in order to build up a picture of his character and preoccupations.

d The narrow-mindedness of the townsfolk in *Lou, the Prophet*, shown in their reaction to his changed appearance and behaviour.

CHARLOTTE BRONTË

Napoleon and   Napoleon Bonaparte, Emperor of France, has retired
the Spectre   for the night. His servant leaves him, having placed a
drink at his side and three lighted candles.

As soon as he is alone, he starts to hear strange noises,
sounding like human voices emanating from a corner
cupboard; then the candles are mysteriously blown out.
The Emperor, being brave, challenges his fear of the
supernatural and brandishes his pistol defiantly in the
direction of the mysterious noises. An apparition
appears, mocking him and showing itself in all its
hideousness. Napoleon is suitably shocked into a
terrified silence.

The spectre constrains Napoleon to follow him, and
they proceed through the walls of the palace and out
into the streets of Paris, Napoleon wearing only his
night things. Eventually they arrive at a grand building
with marble halls, brightly lit for a party. There are
several guests there, all wearing horrible masks.
Napoleon clearly feels extremely uncomfortable and
disorientated at the strange sights and odours
surrounding him.

All of a sudden he catches sight of his wife, Marie

Think whether Louise. Immediately the dreamscape fades and he sees
this spectre is 'real' himself to be in her apartments, where she is throwing
or a figment of a private party for some guests. She informs him that
Napoleon's he appears to have been sleepwalking. His ensuing
imagination. shock renders him unconscious.

COMMENT This is a very strange little tale that was written by
Charlotte Brontë when she was in the very early stages
of her career as a novelist. It highlights her fascination
for the figure of Napoleon, by whom she was captivated
as a girl and romanticised a great deal in the writings of
her youth. The Emperor, leader of the Revolutionary
armies of the French Revolution, widely acclaimed as
one of the greatest military minds in history, would
have been a very dashing figure to the ladies of
nineteenth-century England. Napoleon, with his dark
brooding looks, in fact, became a prototype for the
Romantic (see Literary Terms) hero. His divorce from
his wife and subsequent marriage to the Austrian
princess Marie Louise was also proclaimed as a
romantic story at the time: a nineteenth-century
equivalent to the modern furore over the royal family.

There is a sense here of things uncovered, illicit
meetings, clandestine arrangements, which would have
appealed greatly to the highly impressionable, sheltered
mind of the Brontë sister. It appears odd that the
Emperor's wife is entertaining on rather a grand scale in
the same palace as her husband, and has not invited
him to the gathering. On the contrary, he evidently is
totally unaware of her having guests. Is there an oblique
reference here to marital problems? There is a distinct
sense that Charlotte Brontë is implying separate social
lives and a breakdown in communication between
Napoleon and his wife at the very least.

The echoing corridors, thick castle walls, romantic
heroes, guttering candle flames, spectres and spooks, are

all hallmarks of the best in Gothic (see Literary Terms) fiction, a style popular amongst readers in the early nineteenth century, and satirised (see Literary Terms) by Jane Austen in *Northanger Abbey*. One of the best examples of this form of fiction is *The Mysteries of Udolpho* written by Mrs Radcliffe in 1794.

AMBROSE BIERCE

An Arrest

Bierce tells the story of Orrin Brower, a hardened criminal, who is arrested for killing his brother-in-law. He escapes from jail by knocking down his jailer, the sheriff, with an iron bar, and makes a desperate bid for freedom. His attempt is shadowed by the knowledge that his efforts are undoubtedly doomed to failure, because a 'posse' of local citizens will be hunting for him as soon as his escape is discovered.

Note similarities of style and tone with Hop–Frog; both are bitter, sardonic, abrupt. Bierce's strong admiration for Poe's work is evident.

All of a sudden he comes across the figure of a man, which turns out to be the very same sheriff he had attacked. The figure motions him to retrace his steps. No words are uttered between the two men; Brower realises what his fate will inevitably be if he chooses to ignore the dictates of his silent captor. He turns on his heel and heads back to the jailhouse. Upon opening the door he comes across a group of men surrounding the dead figure of the sheriff himself, laid out upon a table. It was the man's spirit which had pursued him and brought him to justice.

COMMENT

Extremely brief, matter-of-fact and succinct, this is typical of the work of Bierce, who was renowned for his severe depictions of American nineteenth-century life. Its stoic attitude towards violence is also characteristic of his style.

It is interesting to note the contrast between this story and the one preceding it in the anthology; the two could not be more different in tone, style or language.

Whereas Brontë's style is highly descriptive, melodramatic, almost gushy, this is realistic, sardonic and abrupt. It is reminiscent of a news report or other factual account; at certain points it draws attention to its own realism: 'the emotions of the other are not recorded', and 'It is needless to relate them here; they came out at his trial', and so on.

There is a clear moral message to this story, and a sense of inevitability in Brower's capture, albeit by the spirit of the law rather than its physical embodiment. The law is seen to be strong enough to override the constraints of life itself, especially when someone attacks the same embodiment of the law. However, Bierce maintains a tone of admiration for his anti-hero, and praises his bravery and coolness.

GLOSSARY   **posse** America did not have a centralised judicial or policing system; local citizens were often called upon to assist the local law officers in the capture of criminals

SIR ARTHUR CONAN DOYLE

The Adventure of The Speckled Band

This is one of the liveliest, most exciting of the Adventures of Sherlock Holmes. The threat of murder, the arch-villainous figure of Dr Grimesby Roylott, the maiden in distress, all mix in a fabulous melting pot alongside the esteemed characters of Holmes and Dr Watson.

The action begins with the young lady, Helen Stoner, arriving dramatically at Baker Street early one morning, mud-spattered and in a heightened state of anxiety. She begs for assistance from the great 'consulting detective'. It transpires that her life is threatened by her stepfather guardian, the notable Dr Roylott, of whom she is a ward. As she relates her tale to Holmes and Watson, it becomes clear that something very strange has been

going on at Stoke Moran, the home of Roylott and Helen. Her twin sister Julia had died two years previously after becoming engaged to a local young man. Dr Roylott had offered no objection to the marriage, but his violent temper and clear irrationality made the sisters fear him all the same, as he rarely let them out of the house, nor let strangers in to see them.

Shortly after the engagement was announced, it appears that Julia was taken by some strange fit in the night, and died presumably of fright. Helen remembers odd details such as a strange whistling noise and a 'strange metallic sound', and her sister crying out 'the speckled band'. However, no one could uncover any reason for her death.

Helen subsequently became engaged herself, and now fears for her own life. Her stepfather has requested that she take over her dead sister's room, which is directly next to his, and was the scene of her sister's death.

Note how Holmes matches his strength to Roylott's by bending the fire poker, thereby assuring us of his dependability as protector without having to utter a word of boast.

Holmes's curiosity and gentlemanly spirit being aroused, he and Watson travel down to Stoke Moran to solve the mystery. In a dramatic dénouement (see Literary Terms), they uncover Dr Roylott's scheme: the 'Speckled Band' is in fact a swamp adder, a deadly Indian snake, trained by him to descend the bell-rope in the girls' room and bite them. With a characteristic touch of neatness, Roylott is bitten by his own snake and dies instantly. It appears that he was attempting to protect his inheritance by ensuring that the girls did not marry, for if they did, their money would pass to their husbands.

COMMENT   Conan Doyle's hero was popular for many reasons. To Victorian and Edwardian society, he represented all the best of the values they held in high esteem. He was cultured but unpredictable, polite and charming but had hidden depths, was strong and knowledgeable but fallible. He upheld the importance of culture and breeding, and yet mixed among the many layers of London society. Doyle depicted the worst and best of London at that time; the lairs of vice and iniquity, the prostitution and opium dens were referred to openly. However, shielding the innocent characters, the victims, and by association the reader, was the strong and reliable Holmes. No wonder he was so popular. He made it safe to look at the seedier side of life; he was the protector who would deal with the villains and still have a charming word of courtesy for the ladies. Edwardian society had a fear of the 'covered-up' or more primitive elements of human nature. They concentrated upon appearances, etiquette, manners, seemly behaviour, and were terrified of what lay beneath. Holmes was not afraid to plumb those depths. His charm, honesty, dependability and intelligence made him a figure to venerate, a protector. He has been linked to the idea of the classical hero such as Hercules, in a more realistic depiction of the best in human nature.

The popularity of the stories can be judged from their constant reprints and the large amounts sold during Doyle's lifetime.

He was the prototype for the figure of investigating detective which has slipped so comfortably into our present-day culture. Nowadays we have police detectives, private detectives, mystery-writer detectives, pathology detectives, and aristocratic detectives occasionally. However, Holmes was the first great 'consulting detective'. Therefore, the stories of Sherlock Holmes have great significance from a cultural and historical perspective. They can inform the reader of today of much of the preoccupations of the readers of Doyle's era, as well as displaying the first of the genre of detective fiction.

His combination of the pursuit of reason with the employment of intuition have continued to be the primary tools of the fictional detective; for when combined they bring two opposing forces together as a strong weapon.

The considerable length of the story mirrors the deductive process; its detail is essential for the reader to follow the means by which Holmes makes his discoveries and reaches his conclusions. Rather than being involved in this process however, we are barred from the internal process of discovery. Thus we can, like Dr Watson, marvel at the mind which links all the facts together and closes the case.

GLOSSARY   Regency period of British history 1810–20

TEST YOURSELF (Section V)

A *Identify the speaker.*

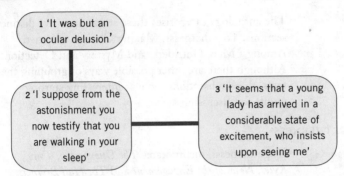

1 'It was but an ocular delusion'

2 'I suppose from the astonishment you now testify that you are walking in your sleep'

3 'It seems that a young lady has arrived in a considerable state of excitement, who insists upon seeing me'

Identify the person 'to whom' this comment refers.

4 Her features and figure were those of a woman of thirty, but her hair was shot with premature gray, and her expression was weary and haggard

5 Turning his back to his captor, he walked submissively away in the direction indicated, looking to neither the right nor the left

Check your answers on page 86.

 B *Consider these issues.*

a How the brevity of *An Arrest* contrasts so strikingly with the detail of *The Speckled Band*.

b How the dialogue and description (see Literary Terms) in Charlotte Brontë's story show it to date from much earlier than the subsequent two stories in the group.

c What elements of the Sherlock Holmes tale show it to be part of an ongoing series, with a central character familiar to readers.

d How all three stories are told from a different perspective to that of the central character.

e The way Dr Watson serves as a useful narrator (see Literary Terms) figure as well as a part of the story.

y

55

PART THREE

COMMENTARY

THEMES

The anthology categorises these stories into five distinct sections; Togetherness?, Making Choices, Women Amongst Men, Outsiders, and Mystery and Detection. Although there are other possible ways of grouping the texts, these subsections serve as interesting starting points for discussion.

TOGETHERNESS?

'Togetherness?' incorporates *The Unexpected, Tony Kytes, News of the Engagement* and *The Half Brothers*. The question mark serves to challenge accepted nineteenth-century attitudes towards familial and marital loyalty. Kate Chopin's story of passion for self-fulfilment introduces the collection with a striking portrayal of one woman's refusal to accept a lifetime's imprisonment married to a man she realises she does not love. The depiction of a passionate woman, strong-willed and desperate, was typical of the characters Kate Chopin created, in her preoccupation with the constraints of Victorian society upon women. She

Compare Victorian attitudes towards women with contemporary expectations.

questioned the apparent necessity for every woman to make a 'good match' for pragmatic reasons, believing that the pursuit of love and passion should be the overriding driving forces. The story highlights similar concerns to those expressed by Charlotte Gilman Perkins in *The Yellow Wallpaper* (see Women Amongst Men below).

Thomas Hardy presents a similar indictment of accepted patterns of betrothal in Tony Kytes; the eponymous (see Literary Terms) hero appears less than contented with his first choice, and only accepts her at all after two others have refused him. His pragmatic attitude towards the necessity of choosing a wife is mirrored by his fiancée, who takes him in spite of being publicly humiliated. The narrator (see Literary Terms) ratifies this attitude by neglecting to pass comment upon their unromantic union, concentrating instead upon the fine party which marks the subsequent marriage; thus sealing the union by a public display of acceptance. This compounds the idea that marriage is a function of duty, a social convention so strong that couples bind to each other under less than satisfactory circumstances rather than defy custom.

We can compare the attitude to our own society's view of marriage. What influenced the nineteenth century to marry and 'settle down'?

There is also a subversive edge to the story which echoes *The Unexpected*. The portrayal of two distinct types of woman is striking, and is clearly an indirect comment upon society's attitudes towards accepted patterns of female behaviour. Negative views are directed towards those women who are assertive; they are judged harshly by society in spite of being favoured by the hero. They also have more self-respect; he is more attracted to them, but loses them because they have too much pride to be treated badly. Milly, however, is more submissive, by allowing Tony to treat her deplorably and still agreeing to marry him. The sense that the two deserve each other is very strong at the end of the story.

The Half Brothers examines the ties of blood and duty; another issue close to the hearts of the Victorians. Despite the sentimental ending, this story is a touching portrayal of the love of one brother for another, and the value and strength of ties of blood and family. The boy Gregory is made into what he is by the cruelty of those around him: a self-fulfilling prophesy, in fact. He suffers from want of love, attention, or respect, and yet maintains a fierce protective love for his younger, perhaps undeserving brother; mindful of the dying wishes of their mother. The young narrator keenly feels his own part in their relationship; how undeserving he is of Gregory's love for him.

Again we see a 'marriage of necessity' which is less common in our society now.

Their mother suffers through marrying for pragmatic reasons rather than romantic ones; she suffers and dies as a result of this choice, but the reader feels sympathy for her and blames the cruelty of a harsh husband rather than judging her for making a wrong decision. This echoes the discussion about marriage raised in *The Unexpected* and *Tony Kytes*.

The ties of loyalty and respect for the wishes of the parent are also highlighted in *News of the Engagement*; however, Bennett's story is far gentler and less dramatic. In one respect it is interesting to note how similar concerns can be addressed in a very different format; although his story appears quite dissimilar in tone and style, there is the exploration of the expectations on both sides from a mother-son relationship. In his story, the son is given the opportunity to mend his ways before an event of any magnitude occurs; he is allowed the dignity of keeping the knowledge of his selfishness to himself. He learns a powerful lesson, however, as does the narrator (see Literary Terms) of *The Half Brothers*. Both authors draw upon the conviction that duty to parents is of paramount importance.

The significance of the issues explored in this section is that they were clearly important to the audience of the time; they highlight concerns about the nature of society's expectations in terms of marriage and duty. Although there were very firm social rules governing all aspects of the choices and responsibility towards family, these stories display an underlying questioning of externally imposed conventions.

MAKING CHOICES

This section draws together three tales strikingly different in tone, subject-matter, setting and cultural concerns. The similarity lies in all three having a choice as the pivotal moment. The choice made by the Vallins is to give their child away in the knowledge that he will receive all the advantages which they, as a poor peasant family, could never dream of providing. They also ensure an income for life. Although castigated by their neighbours for having a flawed value system, their pragmatism eventually bears fruit, whereas the family who stuck by their principles and ideas of family loyalty are punished for their decision to keep their child. As a social and political commentary this story makes uncomfortable reading; the poorest families were often criticised for having large numbers of children whom they struggled to feed. The dilemma of the choice between love for a child and monetary gain is unsettling, and yet the Vallins are proven to have benefited from their pragmatism.

The gentleman in him looks for the best in others.

The hero Van Bibber also has a difficult choice to make, and is similarly rewarded. He trusts the words of a convicted criminal and assists his escape. His choice is motivated by the need to have faith in the best side of human nature. He wants to believe that the criminal has reformed; he also grasps the opportunity to commit a selfless act, which enables him to counteract some of the less inspiring aspects of New York life. He is able to restore his rather shaken faith in the basic decency of human nature by trusting the burglar.

The fairy tale (see Literary Terms) *The Nightingale and the Rose* places romance and philosophy, or the pursuit of learning, in direct opposition to one another. The Student 'chooses' philosophy after being disappointed in love, or rather with love in its abstract sense.

However the Nightingale also chooses; she puts her faith in love and sacrifices herself for that ideal. Her sacrifice is proven to be unappreciated, going totally unnoticed by those for whom it was intended to benefit. Her selfless action shows itself to be misguided in that it is unappreciated, however worthy and altruistic. Her motivation is similar to Van Bibber's in that both actions are performed in pursuit of an ideal.

WOMEN AMONGST MEN

This subheading directly addresses the issue of the patriarchal society of the nineteenth century; women were perceived as subservient figures, with little autonomy and independence. Denied the vote until 1918 in Britain and 1920 in the USA, their choices were limited; marriage was the assumed, expected course for women to take, and working from choice rather than necessity was generally frowned upon.

Women's rights were a very contentious issue at this time.

The political climate with regard to suffrage was heightening in many parts of the world during the late nineteenth century. Olive Schreiner, living in South Africa, fought fiercely for women's rights and wrote *The Woman's Rose* as a comment on the particular value of female mutual support when surrounded by male domination. In her story the two women learn too late that what is valuable in their situation is each other, not the attentions of the men who surround them.

The Yellow Wallpaper gives a powerful depiction of the effects of this powerlessness when driven to extremes. Seen from the internal perspective of depression and eventual insanity, it has a sense of personal experience about it. the narrator (see Literary Terms) is suffering from what would now be referred to as 'post-natal depression'. This is a condition from which the author suffered, and many of the cures suggested to the narrator were also offered to Charlotte Perkins Gilman – cures which she found intolerable. To be told that 'intellectual' pursuits were to be avoided at all costs as being a contributory factor to her illness is a very significant idea in terms of being symptomatic of Victorian attitudes towards women pursuing knowledge. Rebellion against patriarchal imposed authority was an issue explored by more and more women writers of this time.

On both levels, this story is very unsettling; it is a powerful ghost story and a most uncomfortable psychological idea.

The narrator clearly is torn between her loyalty and subservience to her husband and her need to be autonomous; the accepted role of deference to his greater knowledge and experience sits uncomfortably on her shoulders although she does not defy him. However, she knows that it is the imposed confinement of her mind which is driving her insane. The figure behind bars in the wallpaper is herself: a metaphor (see Literary Terms) for her intellectual imprisonment. She is not alone in her suffering; others have behaved similarly in this room. The wallpaper is already torn on their arrival, there are bars on the windows and rings in the walls, which could possibly be to restrain a mad person rather than protect a child. This implies that other women have suffered in the way the narrator is suffering, adding to the social dimension of the point being made by the author, which is that women's potential as intelligent members of society is not utilised. The Victorians had a perception of women as fragile delicate creatures, not strong enough mentally, emotionally or physically for challenging pursuits. Inevitably, in many cases this attitude created just that: a society of women who largely lived up to these expectations. It is no accident of history that the Suffrage movement was born of the Victorian era.

The author in fact uses a device not unfamiliar to other women writers of the nineteenth century. Taking the

conflicting elements of the female personality and
creating two separate characters was used by Charlotte
Brontë in *Jane Eyre*: the meekness embodied in Jane,
the rebellious fiery side displayed by 'the madwoman in
the attic', Bertha. Kate Chopin had used the technique
also in her novel *At Fault*. By the late nineteenth
century there was a more general recognition and
understanding of the New Woman, and that the 'mad'
rebellious woman and 'sane' dutiful woman were in fact
inhabitants of the same body. It was becoming more
acceptable to analyse and explore the troubled female
consciousness in terms of itself and its cultural
surroundings. *The Yellow Wallpaper* attempts to do just
this, in its powerful portrayal of the descent into
madness and eventual fusion of the two female figures.
It employs the device of palimpsest (see Literary
Terms) in order to allow the story to operate on two
levels, the literal supernatural and the figurative
political, thereby ensuring its accessibility to all
readers.

At this time it was still a relatively new idea to explore female psychology in literature.

The woman is not the central figure of *Twenty-six Men
and a Girl*; she is a talisman, a stylised figure created by
desperate men. The central theme (see Literary Terms)
of this story is an exploration of what happens to those
who have little to live for; a comment on humanity's
way of creating illusions and dreams to sustain them.
Gorky questions this tendency, suspecting that the
dream could effectively inhibit men from fully
recognising and fighting against the conditions under
which they were forced to survive.

Russia was, at the time of this story, populated by those
struggling to eke out a meagre existence under terrible
conditions. The Russian Revolution of 1917 was a
direct result of the populace having endured torturous
conditions for too long. Gorky worked alongside the
poorest citizens for many years, and was fascinated by

the way human nature created illusions to sustain their day-to-day lives.

Look for the hints that suggest that Tanya is less than the bakers think of her.

In Tanya, he gives us the portrayal of a vain, frivolous girl who is idealised by those who need to believe in something pure. The rage with which they attack her after she disappoints them shows how deeply they feel betrayed. She has, in effect, destroyed the illusion which sustained them. In fact they know little about her, and judge her far too kindly; she asks many favours and yet is scornful when one of them asks her to darn a shirt. Her value lies solely in the appearance of purity, innocence and beauty; their attitude to her typifies those same attitudes towards women highlighted by other writers. When she displays her true nature they are horrified in their disappointment. Her recognition of this at the end of the story enables her to maintain dignity in the face of violent condemnation.

OUTSIDERS

The four central characters in this group are all on the periphery of the society they inhabit. Dickens's Poor Relation hovers on the outside of the society which in other circumstances he should have comfortably inhabited. This position, however, enables him to be a strong indicter of those who have exacerbated his personal and financial losses. As close observer, tolerated rather than involved, he is near enough to paint a bitterly satirical (see Literary Terms) portrait of the callousness and avarice of others. His position as outsider is preferable to the promised alternative; his dream 'castle' is probably a more comfortable home than dwelling amongst hypocrisy and selfishness.

Lou, the Prophet, is driven to religious fanaticism by despair and lack of acceptance. Lonely and disappointed, his only companions are the local children who accept him for what he is. Dickens, in his story, also focuses on the strength and honesty of children: the Poor Relation's only companion being his young nephew. Lou turns to religion through desperation, and is hounded from the locality for his strange behaviour and appearance. His new-found beliefs actually compound his place on the outskirts of society, however, by enabling him to have the strength to become a total outsider and separate himself totally from his peers rather than attempting to be accepted by them.

Extreme loneliness leads to odd behaviour in all these stories.

The Anarchist in Wells's tale is also on the outskirts of his society; he keenly feels his situation, and is aware that he has always been ignored. His craving for acceptance manifests itself in a bizarre action masquerading as part of an organised plot to overthrow society; however it is patently apparent that the individual is in reality acting purely for his own benefit, staking a place for himself in the annals of history. Years of isolation have driven him to desperation.

These three characters are all outsiders of the society to which they should belong; they all crave acceptance and involvement but are forced to remain on the outskirts. Hop-Frog, however, is an alien to the society he inhabits. Imported against his will, he clearly despises all around him and bears his circumstances with powerless rage until such time as he is able to enact the horrific revenge plot. Far from needing to belong, Hop-Frog wishes to alienate himself from those who have enslaved him. The appalling depiction of him as a monstrous figure is a dramatic reinforcement of society's tendency to shun and mistreat anyone who appears different. Poe creates an exaggerated figure, the effect being to satirise (see Literary Terms), shockingly, human nature's need for uniformity and terror of the uncommon. The idea of the grotesque had an repulsive fascination for Poe's audience, and people would flock to fairs where people suffering from terrible deformities would be displayed on open view. Hop-Frog is an outsider by choice rather than circumstance: a mocking parody of society's rules and prescriptions of conformity.

MYSTERY AND DETECTION

This section concentrates upon the need to preserve order at all costs; to set up mysteries in order to resolve them satisfactorily, thereby maintaining the controlling influences of right and goodness. Charlotte Brontë's strange little Gothic (see Literary Terms) tale is rather a quaint depiction of the nineteenth-century love of melodrama and supernatural forces. The spirit in this story clearly means no harm to Napoleon, and its desire to show the general something important brings to mind the apparitions of Dickens's *A Christmas Carol*. There is a reasonably satisfactory quality to the dénouement (see Literary Terms) for the audience, who can accept that Napoleon merely dreamed up the ghost.

This century loved the supernatural, and were fascinated by ghosts.

The ghost in *An Arrest* has a punitive function. It warns those inhabiting a society still in the early days of formalisation of the weight of the law. The criminal, although hardened and desperate, submits instantly at the sight of what he perceives to be his jailer. The brevity of description and abrupt dénouement (see Literary Terms) highlights the story's function as moral commentator and reminder of the right path to follow.

The popularity of the Sherlock Holmes stories stems partially from similar concerns. The Victorians were living through tremendous social, political and economic changes and welcomed the figure of the brave, righteous, intelligent Holmes as their protector. His position is unequivocal as staunch advocate and protector of the values of truth and morality. It was comforting to have someone battle with mysterious situations and inevitably resolve them satisfactorily.

Although a somewhat 'shady' figure himself on occasion, he was acceptable to readers because he maintained the required societal codes of decorum and civility.

Watch for examples of this need for security and stability, particularly with regard to Sherlock Holmes.

Solving mysteries and reinforcing the security of the natural law was an important idea for societies dominated by change and development. Advances in scientific and rational thinking had redefined the old order and the Victorians were a society struggling at times to come to terms with all the new developments. This need for stability was echoed in their strict moral codes of behaviour, and can even be witnessed visibly, for example in their styles of dress and architecture, where solid, heavy ostentation reinforced metaphorically (see Literary Terms) their place on the earth. The mystery genre, where unexplainable events were unearthed and explained, consolidated this need.

PATTERNS

Although these thematic subsections serve useful functions of categorisation, other themes (see Literary Terms) and ideas equally significant are worth consideration. When considering a collection of stories such as these, their only single point of connection is the era in which they were written, and it would be foolhardy to ignore other patterns and ways of grouping them. For example, the contrast between the concerns and style of the British and American writers highlights differences between an established, powerful society with formalised, centralised codes of behaviour and value systems, and a continent still in the very early days of development, peopled with settlers from around the world, with decentralised government and judiciary. *Lou, the Prophet* and *An Arrest* contrast strikingly with *The Speckled Band, News of the Engagement* and *The Poor Relation's Story* particularly in terms of old versus new society.

Conversely, *The Yellow Wallpaper* displays similar concerns to *The Woman's Rose* and *The Unexpected* in their powerful messages about female suppression: concerns echoed by their transatlantic contemporaries, Charlotte Brontë, George Eliot and others.

The socio-political messages of *Twenty-six Men and a Girl, Country Living* and *The Half Brothers* highlight Russian, French and British dissatisfaction with poverty and inequality. It appears that there was a worldwide concern for the plight of the poor and the unfair distribution of wealth. Issues raised by Maupassant translate easily to British and Irish rural poverty, showing an overriding discontent which communicates easily over cultural barriers.

Industrial Revolution begins in Britain. For the next 100 years people will move from the countryside to industrialised towns	**1750**	
Napoleon becomes Emperor of France	**1804**	
	1809	Birth of Edgar Allan Poe
	1810	Birth of Elizabeth Gaskell
	1812	Birth of Charles Dickens
Battle of Waterloo	**1815**	
	1816	Birth of Charlotte Brontë
Napoleon dies in captivity on St Helena	**1823**	
In Russia an unsuccessful revolt against the Tsar. First railway trains	**1825**	
Industrial Revolution takes effect in France	**1830**	
	1832	
First Reform Bill	**1833**	Charlotte Brontë: **Napoleon and the Spectre**
Britain abolishes Slavery Victoria becomes Queen	**1837**	
Invention of photography	**1840**	Birth of Thomas Hardy
	1842	Birth of Ambrose Bierce
Karl Marx: *Manifesto of Communism.*	**1848**	
Right of women to vote first proposed in United States	**1849**	Edgar Allan Poe: **Hop Frog**
	1850	Birth of Guy de Maupassant
	1852	Charles Dickens: **The Poor Relation's Story**
Crimean War	**1853-6**	
	1854	Birth of Oscar Wilde
	1855	Birth of Olive Schreiner
Charles Darwin publishes *On the Origin of Species*	**1859**	Birth of Arthur Conan Doyle Elizabeth Gaskell: **The Half Brothers**
	1860	Birth of Charlotte Perkins Gilman
Emancipation of Serfs in Russia	**1861**	
American Civil War	**1861-5**	
	1864	Birth of Richard H. Davis

Event	Year	Literary Event
Abraham Lincoln, the American president, assassinated. First bicycle.	**1865**	
	1866	Birth of H.G. Wells
	1867	Birth of Arnold Bennett
	1868	Birth of Maxim Gorky
John Stuart Mill argues for women's right to vote in Britain	**1869**	
Revolutionary Commune in Paris demands economic reforms	**1871**	
First typewriters	**1873**	Birth of Willa Cather
First telephone in use	**1877**	
Assassination of Tsar Alexander II in Russia	**1881**	
	1883	Guy de Maupassant: **Country Living**
Fabian Society founded in England to promote revolutionary socialism	**1884**	
First petrol-driven car	**1885**	
	1888	Oscar Wilde: **The Nightingale and the Rose**
	1890	Olive Schreiner: **The Woman's Rose**
	1891	Ambrose Bierce: **An Arrest**
	1892	Richard H. Davis: **Van Bibber's Burglar.** Charlotte Perkins Gilman: **The Yellow Wallpaper.** Willa Cather: **Lou, the Prophet.** Arthur Conan Doyle: **The Adventure of the Speckled Band**
	1894	H.G. Wells: **The Stolen Bacillus**
The first silent films shown	**1895**	Thomas Hardy: **Tony Kyte, the Arch-Deceiver.** Kate Chopin: **The Unexpected**
	Late **1890s**	Arnold Bennett: **News of the Engagement**
	1899	Maxim Gorky: **26 Men and a Girl**
Death of Queen Victoria	**1901**	
Movement for women's right to vote founded by Mrs Pankhurst	**1903**	
First Russian Revolution	**1905**	
First World War	**1914-18**	
The 'October Revolution' in Russia	**1917**	
Women over 30 granted right to vote	**1918**	
First regular radio broadcasts	**1922**	

Today we accept the short story as a genre in its own right, with an equal place alongside novels, plays and poetry in the rich tapestry of English literature. Stories are studied in schools, more anthologies of them are produced every year, and many modern authors adopt this medium as well as the novel in which to write.

However, before the nineteenth century the short story was perceived as a poor relation to the novel, and in spite of them having been around for many hundreds of years, the genre only fully came into its own during the 1800s. In order to plot the reasons for the rise in popularity, it is necessary to consider the changes in cultural, social and political life which occurred during this century.

Socio-economic events The nineteenth century was a period of rapid and dramatic change for the majority of northern Europe. Before the advent of the Industrial Revolution people had generally worked the land in order to provide for themselves and their families. The greater part of Europe was peopled by 'peasant' classes who farmed for a living, paying rents or taxes to their local landowner. Some trades were in existence, such as blacksmith, wheelwright, carpenter, and so on. Some people were employed by the gentry in service. There was an immense unbridgeable chasm between the working and ruling classes. Cities, such as they were, were small and incomparable to what we recognise as a city today. The majority of the population had very little spare money or time, and worked extremely hard and long hours.

Technological advances However, the invention of the internal combustion engine marked the dramatic change from this way of life. More efficient means of production, generated by technological advances, caused factories to shoot up over Europe. The rural population flocked into the cities, where the majority of the factories were located, in order to seek employment. This provoked a period of terrible poverty and extremely harsh conditions, with many factory owners exploiting their workers with poor pay, very long hours and dangerous work on heavy machinery. Children as young as four were given a pittance to work in the huge mills. The mortality rate was high and people were poor.

Demand for better working conditions

This situation changed as people demanded a better working environment, and banded together to form the first trade unions. These first unions were a very powerful force and ensured good pay and reasonable working conditions for all. By the mid-nineteenth century, although people were still faced with hardship, things had improved. Health-care plans and insurances became more common, and co-operatives were set up to support the working classes financially.

Educational advances

One benefit of the unions was the setting up of factory schools, where some factory owners allowed the children of their workers to be educated in basic literacy and numeracy. The cultural implications of this were immense, as generally only the children of the most well-off had previously been formally educated, either at home with a tutor/governess or at boarding school. The literacy rates soared, and the perception of the value of getting a basic education increased. At the beginning of the nineteenth century, the importance of reading was perceived only in terms of the moral education of children; that is, if one could read, then one could read the Bible. However, by the mid-1800s, it was recognised that there was great value in pursuing ideas and learning to assist rational thought and knowledge. Reading came to be valued not just as a means to aid religious instruction, but to enable individuals to learn for learning's sake.

The printing revolution

Advances in methods and techniques of printing, also influenced by the industrial revolution, enabled there to be increased accessibility of reading matter. Publishing houses were set up, and many newspapers and magazines flourished from the cheaper production of the written word and greater demand from a far more literate public.

Magazine and newspaper serialisation

The short story found its ideal home in magazines and newspapers. Authors found this medium an excellent way of earning money and reaching a wider audience than by the publication of novels. Charles Dickens used his own magazine in order to serialise his novels, which shows in the way they generally are structured in distinct units with exciting events to keep the reader interested and wanting more, much akin to the modern soap opera. All the authors in this collection wrote for magazines and newspapers, and many preferred this medium to that of the more unwieldy novel format.

Reading as a social pastime

Above all, the cultural attitude to reading changed. It became a social pastime, and families would group together in the evenings, prior to the advent of radio and TV, to listen to the reading of a short story. The structure and format of them allowed them to be accessible and reach a wide audience. Thus subgenres quickly developed and soon came to be recognised as familiar; mystery, horror, supernatural, romance were particularly popular in the nineteenth century. *The Poor Relation's Story* and *Tony Kytes, the Arch-Deceiver* both highlight the use of story as entertainment with their openings, which draw attention to the narrative stance of the tale.

There are marked features which identify a short story as a genre separate from other forms of prose fiction. Most stories need to contain certain specific elements in order to be categorised as such.

Length

The length of a story is obvious and significant. Many writers adopt the genre of short story because it allows them to explore ideas and issues within a format which is relatively flexible and easy to manage. A novel tends to demand an identity of its own, with details of place, setting and character vital to the maintenance of the storyline. A short story need contain none of the above, or maybe one or two. It can be used to comment upon a theme, or relay an anecdotal (see Literary Terms) incident, or present a cameo of character. It is complete in its own right; there need be no chapter breaks or subsections. There is concentration upon one theme, event or person, rather than the subplots which tend to occur in novels. It tends towards succinctness, and the plots are not elaborate. A climax is essential, and there will be no long build up to it nor lengthy elaboration afterwards.

Characters

Although the short story is similar to the novel in its use of characterisation, one of the most distinct differences between the story and the novel is that the characters do not have space to become fully rounded, developed individuals; therefore, they tend to be used in stories in order to display qualities or traits of human nature.

'Twist in the tail'

Because of the need to create a sense of completeness about the short story, it is not unusual for them to have strong endings; either a 'twist in the tale' or dramatic event to give a sense of closure (see Literary Terms) and roundness. Because many were published initially for a magazine or newspaper audience, they needed to present a strong sense of finality in order to appeal to their mass readership. They also begin purposefully, taking no time introducing the reader to the events and circumstances concerned. There is no necessity to develop lengthy, detailed introductions.

Exploration of ideas

The story was used to explore political, social and moral ideas; they can be studied in order to access concerns of a previous century. Previous discussion (see The Historical Perspective of the Story) has shown how writers employed this genre as a means of commenting on their own cultural and social world. Present-day writers utilise the story medium in similar ways, however; for example science fiction (see Literary Terms) has been described as a way of commenting on concerns about the present by looking to the future.

Time span

The majority of the stories in this collection have as their central feature an event, which is described in more or less detail depending on the personal style of the writer concerned, and the fashion of their particular time. The time-span of each story is relatively short; a few days or weeks maybe, or hours in some cases. Only *Country Living* and *The Half Brothers* span years from start to finish of the tale, and even they are mainly concerned with one central incident or event.

Some events are quite dramatic, whilst others merely focus on a moment in an 'ordinary' life.

The Poor Relation's Story is slightly different: it draws attention to its own narrative nature with the anecdotal (see Literary Terms) introduction, but then goes on to relay the events surrounding the narrator's (see Literary Terms) life in a very similar manner to that adopted by Dickens in his novels. In fact, this story can almost be described as a condensed version of one of his novels, without the immense attention to detail and subplots which tend to pepper his work. Therefore, the twist at the end is important in order to give a sense of finality to the story.

As a way of studying particular features of language and style employed by the authors in this collection, it is useful to compile and compare details of chronology (see Literary Terms), cultural background and publishing history. For example, the five American authors have a style most distinct from that of the English authors of earlier in the century. In particular, *An Arrest* by Ambrose Bierce can be contrasted with Charlotte Brontë's *Napoleon and the Spectre* for their marked differences in tone, style and language. His curt, reporting style of narration contrasts to her formal, expressive use of descriptive language. His was the style of an American journalist of the late 1800s, hers of an English novelist of the early part of that century.

Look specifically at the use of descriptive language.

Of the eight English stories, three precede the mid-1800s – *The Half Brothers*, *The Poor Relation's Story* and *Napoleon and the Spectre*. The three authors, Dickens, Gaskell and Brontë were all renowned novelists and chose that form for much of their work.

The stories have distinct similarities which mark them as alike despite the circumstantial details, however. They tend towards a formality of tone and descriptive language which shows them to be earlier than others in the collection. For example, Charlotte Brontë's use of dialogue (see Literary Terms) is extremely formal almost stuffy:

> 'Mon Dieu!' exclaimed the Emperor, 'what do I see? Spectre, whence cometh thou?'
>   The apparition spoke not, but gliding forward beckoned Napoleon with uplifted finger to follow. (p. 156).

The Poor Relation's Story displays similar points of formality, with long sentences, complicated vocabulary and grammatical constructions:

He was very reluctant to take precedence of so many respected members of the family, by beginning the round of stories they were to relate as they sat in a goodly circle by the Christmas fire; and he modestly suggested that it would be more correct if 'John our esteemed host' (whose health he begged to drink) would have the kindness to begin (p. 115).

Mrs Gaskell writes in an equally formal way, employing antiquated expressions and similarly complex grammatical constructions:

I was too dull, too selfish, too numb to think and reason, or I might have known that in that bleak bare place there was naught to wrap me in, save what was taken off another. I was glad enough when he ceased his cares and lay down by me. I took his hand.

Note the sentence length and use of subordinate clauses here. Also the use of 'archaic' words.

'Thou canst not remember, lad, how we lay together thus by our dying mother. She put thy small, wee hand in mine – reckon she sees us now; and belike we shall soon be with her. Anyhow, God's will be done' (p. 42).

Other interesting comparisons may be made with other groupings, for example the differences between the French and Russian stories and the English or American. Also, the writers, who were predominantly journalists such as Harding Davies and Bierce, adopt a very matter-of-fact narrative style, whereas the novelists and prose fiction writers tend towards close attention to detailed descriptive language. The more straightforward, forthright approach of those stories written at the end of the century highlights the more outward-looking, dynamic way of viewing the world and exploring the cultural and social changes occurring; this attitude caused the last decade to be often referred to as 'The Roaring Nineties'.

PART FOUR

Study skills

How to use quotations

One of the secrets of success in writing essays is the way you use quotations. There are five basic principles:

- Put inverted commas at the beginning and end of the quotation
- Write the quotation exactly as it appears in the original
- Do not use a quotation that repeats what you have just written
- Use the quotation so that it fits into your sentence
- Keep the quotation as short as possible

Quotations should be used to develop the line of thought in your essays.

Your comment should not duplicate what is in the quotation. For example:

> The description of Tony Kytes in the first paragraph tells us that his face is small and scarred by smallpox, "Twas a little, round, firm, tight face, with a seam here and there left by the smallpox, but not enough to hurt his looks in a woman's eye.'

Far more effective is to write:

> The introductory information about Tony Kytes describes his face as having 'a seam here and there left by the smallpox, but not enough to hurt his looks in a woman's eye'.

However, the most sophisticated way of using the writer's words is to embed them into your sentence:

> In spite of the preliminary troubles, the couple have a 'fine party' to mark their eventual wedding.

When you use quotations in this way, you are demonstrating the ability to use text as evidence to support your ideas - not simply including words from the original to prove you have read it.

Everyone writes differently. Work through the suggestions given here and adapt the advice to suit your own style and interests. This will improve your essay-writing skills and allow your personal voice to emerge.

The following points indicate in ascending order the skills of essay writing:
- Picking out one or two facts about the story and adding the odd detail
- Writing about the text by retelling the story
- Retelling the story and adding a quotation here and there
- Organising an answer which explains what is happening in the text and giving quotations to support what you write

....

- Writing in such a way as to show that you have thought about the intentions of the writer of the text and that you understand the techniques used
- Writing at some length, giving your viewpoint on the text and commenting by picking out details to support your views
- Looking at the text as a work of art, demonstrating clear critical judgement and explaining to the reader of your essay how the enjoyment of the text is assisted by literary devices, linguistic effects and psychological insights; showing how the text relates to the time when it was written

The dotted line above represents the division between lower- and higher-level grades. Higher-level performance begins when you start to consider your response as a reader of the text. The highest level is reached when you offer an enthusiastic personal response and show how this piece of literature is a product of its time.

Coursework   Set aside an hour or so at the start of your work to plan
essay   what you have to do.

- List all the points you feel are needed to cover the task. Collect page references of information and quotations that will support what you have to say. A helpful tool is the highlighter pen: this saves painstaking copying and enables you to target precisely what you want to use.
- Focus on what you consider to be the main points of the essay. Try to sum up your argument in a single sentence, which could be the closing sentence of your essay. Depending on the essay title, it could be a statement about a character:Sherlock Holmes displays all the qualities a Victorian audience would admire; an opinion about a setting: the claustrophobic, depressing environment of *Twenty-six Men and a Girl* is an essential element in adding to the desperation of the men; or a judgement on a theme: the theme of 'outsiders' shows particularly well in *The Poor Relation's Story*, as Michael is close enough to each character really to appreciate his loneliness and loss of position.
- Make a short essay plan. Use the first paragraph to introduce the argument you wish to make. In the following paragraphs develop this argument with details, examples and other possible points of view. Sum up your argument in the last paragraph. Check you have answered the question.
- Write the essay, remembering all the time the central point you are making.
- On completion, go back over what you have written to eliminate careless errors and improve expression. Read it aloud to yourself, or, if you are feeling more confident, to a relative or friend.

If you can, try to type your essay using a word processor. This will allow you to correct and improve your writing without spoiling its appearance.

Examination
essay

The essay written in an examination often carries more marks than the coursework essay even though it is written under considerable time pressure.

In the revision period build up notes on various aspects of the text you are using. Fortunately, in acquiring this set of York Notes on *Nineteenth Century Short Stories*, you have made a prudent beginning! York Notes are set out to give you vital information and help you to construct your personal overview of the text.

Make notes with appropriate quotations about the key issues of the set text. Go into the examination knowing your text and having a clear set of opinions about it.

In most English Literature examinations you can take in copies of your set books. This in an enormous advantage although it may lull you into a false sense of security. Beware! There is simply not enough time in an examination to read the book from scratch.

In the
examination

- Read the question paper carefully and remind yourself what you have to do.
- Look at the questions on your set texts to select the one that most interests you and mentally work out the points you wish to stress.
- Remind yourself of the time available and how you are going to use it.
- Briefly map out a short plan in note form that will keep your writing on track and illustrate the key argument you want to make.
- Then set about writing it.
- When you have finished, check through to eliminate errors.

To summarise,
these are the
keys to success

- **Know the text**
- **Have a clear understanding of and opinions on the storyline, characters, setting, themes and writer's concerns**
- **Select the right material**
- **Plan and write a clear response, continually bearing the question in mind**

A typical essay question on *Nineteenth Century Short Stories* is followed by a sample essay plan in note form. This does not present the only answer to the question, merely one answer. Do not be afraid to include your own ideas, and leave out some of those in the sample! Remember that quotations are essential to prove and illustrate the points you make.

The section 'Women Amongst Men' highlights concerns with representations of the changing roles of women at this time. Choose two other stories which also address this issue, and discuss the way it is presented.

Introduction   Address the question; look at the section highlighted, mention the stories within, briefly gloss their relevance to the question. Two other stories – *The Unexpected* and *Tony Kytes*, perhaps? Briefly say why (both have as essential elements views of the roles of women in their society; also women breaking out of those roles).

Part 1   Look in more detail at each of the three stories in the 'Women Amongst Men' section. Taking one at a time, discuss the role of women in each; for example, *The Woman's Rose* shows two women prized and fought over for their physical appearance and demure conduct. The women value this male attention more than the friendship and support they could have from each other. The message of the story is that the friendship of women is more sustaining and permanent than the affections of a man. In *The Yellow Wallpaper*, the narrator is driven to insanity by not being allowed to pursue her creative talents and abilities. By being shut away and treated as something delicate, she is driven mad. In *Twenty-six Men and a Girl*, the men value the woman for her physical attributes, but they go further and invent an identity for her, which they are furious with her for when she shows herself to be different.

(Use one good quotation from each story to highlight the message.)

Part 2 Bring in the other two stories. Discuss them in turn. *The Unexpected* shows a woman driven to despair when she realises that she does not love the man she is to marry. Discuss why that would be so terrible, why she should have to marry at all, etc. Go through the story, picking out the bits where she is told what to do, either by society, her parents, or whatever. She is not in control of her own life because she is a woman.

Why would the story be shocking? Mention the fact that it deals with the idea of female desire, and taking control and being forthright. This would not be a popular idea to the Victorians.

In Tony Kytes, mention the differences between the two other women and Milly. Who are the more attractive characters? Who are the strongest? Who does Tony deserve? Look at the reaction of Tony's father; of whom does he not approve?

(Remember again to quote where necessary, to highlight points and display clear understanding of the text.)

Conclusion Draw together the stories with a wider perspective. Mention attitudes to women at that time, and how they are reflected in the stories you have discussed. You can say here that Chopin was dismissed as vulgar and shocking, and that Gilman chose to write her story to be perceived on two levels, the literal and the metaphorical (see Literary Terms), to make it more palatable to the Victorian audience. Finally, how do you rate their effectiveness as barometers of attitudes to women in the nineteenth century? Do you like/dislike them? Why?

1 Compare and contrast the use of setting in three of the stories in this anthology.

2 Discuss the ways in which Ambrose Bierce's *An Arrest* can fit into the same definition of the short story as *The Adventure of the Speckled Band*.

3 'An essential element of a short story is the climax.' Discuss this statement in the light of two stories from the anthology.

4 The nineteenth century was a time of unrest and upheaval in many respects. Choose three of the stories which reflect the changing times, and discuss the ways in which this is represented.

PART FIVE

CULTURAL CONNECTIONS

BROADER PERSPECTIVES

Short stories have an advantage over novels: they are practical; they do not take long to read and are very user-friendly in terms of presenting a fully rounded piece of literature in an immediate way. Charles Dickens presented many of his novels in a serialised format in his magazine *Household Words*. He recognised that readers liked the instantaneous enjoyment they could get from a short piece of story.

Modern-day media also recognise this. Compare some television soap operas and see how they use plot and structure. There is invariably one main plotline or event in each, although the wider issues, characters and storylines need to run through every episode in order to keep the audience glued.

For an example of a composite modern storyteller, look at some collections of stories by Roald Dahl, or Steven King (one in particular called *Night Shift*). These authors work in exactly the same way as writers of the nineteenth century, presenting a clear plot, event, climax and often a 'twist in the tale'. There are also lots of collections of ghost stories, mystery and detection stories, and collections of stories by women writers which you may find interesting.

To get a better flavour of the nineteenth century, try *Great Expectations* by Charles Dickens, *Jane Eyre* by Charlotte Brontë, or *Tess of the D'Urbervilles* by Thomas Hardy.

anecdotes narratives of small incidents or events

atmosphere a common though vague word for the mood which dominates a piece of writing

caricature a grotesque or ludicrous rendering of character, achieved by exaggerating personality traits

chronology time sequence of a list of events

closure the impression of completeness and finality achieved by the ending of the work, particularly relevant to short stories

context the surrounding ideas, setting or words to give a piece of literature its meaning

description the creation or representation in words of objects, people, behaviour or scenes

dénouement final unknotting of a plot

dialogue speech and conversation of characters in any kind of literary work

documentary a reconstruction of an event in an exact historical rather than imaginative manner

empathy/empathise total involvement with the object of sympathy

eponymous taking the name of the title

fairy tale imaginary creatures, supernatural elements interacting with ordinary people

Gothic dealing with cruel passions and supernatural terrors in some mediaeval setting, such as a castle

irony saying one thing whilst meaning another, in order to achieve meaning by understatement, concealment and allusion

legend a story about a heroic personage, such as Robin Hood

literal the most precise and limited meaning

metaphor(ical) a deep meaning, an implied rather than direct meaning

narrator the person telling the story. An 'omniscient' narrator is outside the action, and can see into the minds of the characters. A first-person narrator tells the story as he or she sees it, using 'I'.

palimpsest an occasional use of this term is to describe a piece of text which has a literal and subliteral meaning

Romantic period 1789–1830 (ish) in European literary history

satire writing that examines vice and folly and makes them appear ridiculous through humour

science fiction stories of imaginary marvels or disasters created by future worlds

subtext a word for any implicit assumptions or situation that can be discerned behind the manifest and explicit plot of a story

theme the abstract subject of a work; its central idea or ideas rather than plot or story

vernacular the language of one's homeland, or rough, earthy speech

Victorian period the reign of Queen Victoria, 1837–1901

Test yourself (Sect. I: Togetherness?)

A 1 Dorothea *(The Unexpected)*
2 Tony Kytes *(Tony Kytes, the Arch-Deceiver)*
3 Philip *(News of the Engagement)*
4 Gregory *(The Half Brothers)*
5 Gregory *(The Half Brothers)*
6 Tony Kytes

Test yourself (Sect. II: Making choices)

A 1 Madame Tuvache *(Country Living)*
2 Charlot Tuvache *(Country Living)*
3 Van Bibber *(Van Bibber's Burglar)*
4 The Student *(The Nightingale and the Rose)*
5 The Nightingale *(The Nightingale and the Rose)*
6 Madame Tuvache
7 Van Bibber

Test yourself (Sect. III: Women Amongst Men)

A 1 The fair-haired lady of *The Woman's Rose*
2 The narrator of *The Yellow Wallpaper*

3 The Soldier *(Twenty-six Men and a Girl)*
4 Tanya *(Twenty-six Men and a Girl)*
5 Tanya
6 The fair-haired lady of *The Woman's Rose*

Test yourself (Sect. IV: Outsiders)

A 1 Michael *(The Poor Relation's Story)*
2 Lou, the Prophet
3 The Anarchist *(The Stolen Bacillus)*
4 Michael's uncle *(The Poor Relation's Story)*
5 Hop-Frog
6 The Bacteriologist *(The Stolen Bacillus)*

Test yourself (Sect. V: Mystery and Detection)

A 1 Napoleon *(Napoleon and the Spectre)*
2 Marie Louise *(Napoleon and the Spectre)*
3 Sherlock Holmes
4 Helen Stoner *(The Speckled Band)*
5 Orrin Brower *(An Arrest)*

y

NOTES

NOTES

NOTES

NOTES

GCSE and equivalent levels (£3.50 each)

Harold Brighouse
Hobson's Choice

Charles Dickens
Great Expectations

Charles Dickens
Hard Times

George Eliot
Silas Marner

William Golding
Lord of the Flies

Thomas Hardy
The Mayor of Casterbridge

Susan Hill
I'm the King of the Castle

Barry Hines
A Kestrel for a Knave

Harper Lee
To Kill a Mockingbird

Arthur Miller
A View from the Bridge

Arthur Miller
The Crucible

George Orwell
Animal Farm

J.B. Priestley
An Inspector Calls

J.D. Salinger
The Catcher in the Rye

William Shakespeare
Macbeth

William Shakespeare
The Merchant of Venice

William Shakespeare
Romeo and Juliet

William Shakespeare
Twelfth Night

George Bernard Shaw
Pygmalion

John Steinbeck
Of Mice and Men

Mildred D. Taylor
Roll of Thunder, Hear My Cry

James Watson
Talking in Whispers

A Choice of Poets

Nineteenth Century Short Stories

Poetry of the First World War

Advanced level (£3.99 each)

Margaret Atwood
The Handmaid's Tale

Jane Austen
Emma

Jane Austen
Pride and Prejudice

William Blake
Poems/Songs of Innocence and Songs of Experience

Emily Brontë
Wuthering Heights

Geoffrey Chaucer
Wife of Bath's Prologue and Tale

Joseph Conrad
Heart of Darkness

Charles Dickens
Great Expectations

F. Scott Fitzgerald
The Great Gatsby

Thomas Hardy
Tess of the D'Urbervilles

Seamus Heaney
Selected Poems

James Joyce
Dubliners

William Shakespeare
Antony and Cleopatra

William Shakespeare
Hamlet

William Shakespeare
King Lear

William Shakespeare
Macbeth

William Shakespeare
Othello

Mary Shelley
Frankenstein

Alice Walker
The Color Purple

John Webster
The Duchess of Malfi

FUTURE TITLES IN THE YORK NOTES SERIES

Chinua Achebe
Things Fall Apart

Edward Albee
Who's Afraid of Virginia Woolf?

Jane Austen
Mansfield Park

Jane Austen
Northanger Abbey

Jane Austen
Persuasion

Jane Austen
Sense and Sensibility

Samuel Beckett
Waiting for Godot

John Betjeman
Selected Poems

Robert Bolt
A Man for All Seasons

Charlotte Brontë
Jane Eyre

Robert Burns
Selected Poems

Lord Byron
Selected Poems

Geoffrey Chaucer
The Franklin's Tale

Geoffrey Chaucer
The Knight's Tale

Geoffrey Chaucer
The Merchant's Tale

Geoffrey Chaucer
The Miller's Tale

Geoffrey Chaucer
The Nun's Priest's Tale

Geoffrey Chaucer
The Pardoner's Tale

Geoffrey Chaucer
Prologue to the Canterbury Tales

Samuel Taylor Coleridge
Selected Poems

Daniel Defoe
Moll Flanders

Daniel Defoe
Robinson Crusoe

Shelagh Delaney
A Taste of Honey

Charles Dickens
Bleak House

Charles Dickens
David Copperfield

Charles Dickens
Oliver Twist

Emily Dickinson
Selected Poems

John Donne
Selected Poems

Douglas Dunn
Selected Poems

George Eliot
Middlemarch

George Eliot
The Mill on the Floss

T.S. Eliot
The Waste Land

T.S. Eliot
Selected Poems

Henry Fielding
Joseph Andrews

E.M. Forster
Howards End

E.M. Forster
A Passage to India

John Fowles
The French Lieutenant's Woman

Elizabeth Gaskell
North and South

Oliver Goldsmith
She Stoops to Conquer

Graham Greene
Brighton Rock

Graham Greene
The Heart of the Matter

Graham Greene
The Power and the Glory

Thomas Hardy
Far from the Madding Crowd

Thomas Hardy
Jude the Obscure

Thomas Hardy
The Return of the Native

Thomas Hardy
Selected Poems

L.P. Hartley
The Go-Between

Nathaniel Hawthorne
The Scarlet Letter

Ernest Hemingway
A Farewell to Arms

Ernest Hemingway
The Old Man and the Sea

Homer
The Iliad

Homer
The Odyssey

Gerard Manley Hopkins
Selected Poems

Ted Hughes
Selected Poems

Aldous Huxley
Brave New World

Henry James
Portrait of a Lady

Ben Jonson
The Alchemist

Ben Jonson
Volpone

James Joyce
A Portrait of the Artist as a Young Man

John Keats
Selected Poems

Philip Larkin
Selected Poems

D.H. Lawrence
The Rainbow

D.H. Lawrence
Selected Stories

D.H. Lawrence
Sons and Lovers

D.H. Lawrence
Women in Love

Laurie Lee
Cider with Rosie

Christopher Marlowe
Doctor Faustus

Arthur Miller
Death of a Salesman

John Milton
Paradise Lost Bks I & II

John Milton
Paradise Lost IV & IX

Sean O'Casey
Juno and the Paycock

George Orwell
Nineteen Eighty-four

FUTURE TITLES (continued)

John Osborne
Look Back in Anger

Wilfred Owen
Selected Poems

Harold Pinter
The Caretaker

Sylvia Plath
Selected Works

Alexander Pope
Selected Poems

Jean Rhys
Wide Sargasso Sea

William Shakespeare
As You Like It

William Shakespeare
Coriolanus

William Shakespeare
Henry IV Pt 1

William Shakespeare
Henry IV Pt II

William Shakespeare
Henry V

William Shakespeare
Julius Caesar

William Shakespeare
Measure for Measure

William Shakespeare
Much Ado About Nothing

William Shakespeare
A Midsummer Night's Dream

William Shakespeare
Richard II

William Shakespeare
Richard III

William Shakespeare
Sonnets

William Shakespeare
The Taming of the Shrew

William Shakespeare
The Tempest

William Shakespeare
The Winter's Tale

George Bernard Shaw
Arms and the Man

George Bernard Shaw
Saint Joan

Richard Brinsley Sheridan
The Rivals

R.C. Sherriff
Journey's End

Muriel Spark
The Prime of Miss Jean Brodie

John Steinbeck
The Grapes of Wrath

John Steinbeck
The Pearl

Tom Stoppard
Rosencrantz and Guildenstern are Dead

Jonathan Swift
Gulliver's Travels

John Millington Synge
The Playboy of the Western World

W.M. Thackeray
Vanity Fair

Mark Twain
Huckleberry Finn

Virgil
The Aeneid

Derek Walcott
Selected Poems

Oscar Wilde
The Importance of Being Earnest

Tennessee Williams
Cat on a Hot Tin Roof

Tennessee Williams
The Glass Menagerie

Tennessee Williams
A Streetcar Named Desire

Virginia Woolf
Mrs Dalloway

Virginia Woolf
To the Lighthouse

William Wordsworth
Selected Poems

W.B. Yeats
Selected Poems

York Notes – the Ultimate Literature Guides

York Notes are recognised as the best literature study guides.
If you have enjoyed using this book and have found it useful, you
can now order others directly from us – simply follow the ordering
instructions below.

HOW TO ORDER

Decide which title(s) you require and then order in one of the following ways:

Booksellers
All titles available from good bookstores.

By post
List the title(s) you require in the space provided overleaf, select your method of payment, complete your name and address details and return your completed order form and payment to:

Addison Wesley Longman Ltd
PO BOX 88
Harlow
Essex CM19 5SR

By phone
Call our Customer Information Centre on 01279 623923 to place your order, quoting mail number: HEYN1.

By fax
Complete the order form overleaf, ensuring you fill in your name and address details and method of payment, and fax it to us on 01279 414130.

By e-mail
E-mail your order to us on awlhe.orders@awl.co.uk listing title(s) and quantity required and providing full name and address details as requested overleaf. Please quote mail number: HEYN1. Please do not send credit card details by e-mail.

York Notes Order Form

Titles required:

Quantity	Title/ISBN	Price

Sub total _____

Please add £2.50 postage & packing _____

(*P & P is free for orders over £50*) _____

Total _____

Mail no: HEYN1

Your Name _____

Your Address _____

_____

Postcode _____ Telephone _____

Method of payment

☐ I enclose a cheque or a P/O for £_____ made payable to Addison Wesley Longman Ltd

☐ Please charge my Visa/Access/AMEX/Diners Club card
Number _____ Expiry Date _____
Signature _____ Date _____

(please ensure that the address given above is the same as for your credit card)

Prices and other details are correct at time of going to press but may change without notice. All orders are subject to status.

☐ *Please tick this box if you would like a complete listing of Longman Study Guides (suitable for GCSE and A-level students)*

🌐 York Press

🏛 Longman

Addison Wesley Longman